MY GREEK KETO KITCHEN

GREEK RECIPES WITH A KETO TWIST

LOW – CARB + PRIMAL + PALEO

LIFESTYLE ~ FRIENDLY

By Maria Hatzimarkos

*Foreword by **Jimmy Moore***

Published by:
Maria Hatzimarkos,
Owner & Founder of
Your KeToRRific Journey

Registration No. 1183983
Canadian Intellectual Property Office / An operating agency of the Canadian Goverment
Copyright 2021 © by Maria Hatzimarkos

Copy Editing by: Lucy Topetta, Illuminate The Page
Proof Reading by: Cyntha Jan, Cynthia Jan Health - Certified Nutritional Practitioner & Naturopath
Photographs by: Laura Lee Peters
Book Cover and Recipe Index Design by: Donna M Sullivan
Illustrations (mascots) by: Hedri, healivio.studio - Graphic Designer

ISBN: 978-1-7778148-0-9

Dedication/ Thank You

To My Mother: Thank you for inspiring me with your passion for cooking and baking. As a little girl, I stood in awe of your skills and loved the way you taught me all the tips and tricks from the Greek kitchen, with a wink and a smile. Thank you for sharing with me our family recipes passed down from generations, and for your continuous support from as far away as our beloved Greece.

To My Husband Tony: To the man in our household who started all of this, thank you for your unending love, support and dedication. This book was born from the desire to share your personal success in reaching challenging health goals and how we adopted your methods as a family.   If it were not for you taking charge of your own health, we would not be here in this moment creating a healthy lifestyle as a family, and inspiring others to do the same.

To My Boys, Dimitri and George: My biggest WHY is both of you. I embarked on this journey in the hopes that I could show you what making and eating "real" food looks like, and to pave a path for you towards a future of healthy food choices. Thank you for your patience when I spent endless days in the kitchen cooking and testing. Thank you for being my Main Testers and hardest critics as I know your love of food is even bigger than mine. Your feedback has been of immeasurable value to all the recipes in this book.

Beyond my family, there are a few people I need to thank – Lucy, Laura, Cynthia, Lina, Natalie, Mariam, Anne-Marie, Darlene, Irini and Jackie. As you were my number one supporters, motivating and guiding me along the way - and in many ways, I thank you from the bottom of my heart. If not for you, this book may not have seen the light. Thank you for your help, guidance and friendship!

Finally, a huge thank you goes to all of my KeToRRific clients. Thank you for allowing me to share my story with you and for your continuous support and encouragement. Sharing your stories and health goals with me is what keeps me motivated and focused. It also inspires me to move forward and to learn more so I can share more. This book is for all of you who love Greek traditional meals and the Keto Lifestyle! I sincerely hope that our favourite Greek family recipes inspire you to create in your own Keto kitchen. My deepest wish is that you learn to enjoy the best of Greek cooking without the guilt and stay on track with your Keto lifestyle.

Cheering You on Your KeToRRific Journey!
Much Love,
Maria

DISCLAIMER

This book, or parts thereof, may not be reproduced in any form without permission from the author. Exceptions may be made for brief excerpts used in published reviews, with prior approval.

Any application of the recommendations mentioned in this book are at the reader's discretion and own risk. The information and advice provided in this book has not been evaluated by the U.S. Food and Drug Administration, nor any other organization. The contents of this book should not be used to diagnose or treat any illness, disease or health problem. Always consult your physician, doctor or health care provider before beginning any weight, nutrition or exercise program.

The material contained in this book is provided for educational and informational purposes only and is not intended as medical advice. This book does not attempt to replace any diet or instructions from your doctor.
The author of this book is not a doctor or health professional. The information and opinions expressed in this book are believed to be accurate, based on the best judgment available to the author. In addition, the author does not represent or warrant that the information available in this book is complete or up to date.

The nutritional data listed for each recipe has been calculated in accordance with an online application called CRONOMETER © (https://cronometer.com/). While the author cannot guarantee absolute accuracy of every item, every possible attempt has been made to ensure the quality of the data provided.

Nutritional information provided is only to be used as a guide and may vary due to brands, products, or diet programs used. It is recommended that you calculate your own nutritional macros to suit your needs. Please seek professional healthcare or medical advice before making any dietary changes. Neither the publisher or the author take any responsibility for any possible consequences of any person reading or following any information in this book.

Your use of this book confirms that you are in agreement with the above terms and conditions.

CONTENTS

RECIPES

FOREWORD

When I was writing my book *"Keto Clarity"* in 2013 long before the low-carb, high-fat diet became popular in the mainstream, I had visions that someday soon it would encompass not just the parameters of the diet that induces a state of nutritional ketosis to get all the myriad of health benefits. My hope and dream would be that it would be so embraced as the healthy way of eating that it is that it could cross over into literally any cuisine you want from around the world.

To my delight, that's exactly what has unfolded over the past decade and creative cooks from around the world are making keto options available for their traditional favourite ethnic foods. So when I found out that Maria Hatzimarkos was writing a keto cookbook for the Greek cuisine, I could barely contain my excitement and delight. This book you have in your hands right now is many years in the making, but it could not come at a better time if you are looking to fully optimize your weight and health.

Maria shares why she is so passionate about the ketogenic lifestyle and how she makes it fit within her Greek culture as well as her health goals. She does an incredible job of explaining what healthy fats and proteins are and why they are so vitally important for you to get when you go on the keto diet. And unlike the common misperception that people have about keto, there are indeed healthy carbohydrates included that Maria explains in this book. As a longtime keto dieter, educator, and author, I was very pleased with the simplicity of how she presented this sometimes confusing information. You're gonna love it!

Because the Greek dishes you will be making may be a little different than other recipes you have made in the past, Maria arms you with specific tools, ingredients, and tips for success that will make sure your meals turn out exactly the way you wanted them to. That's such an invaluable resource when you're trying something new—but it's also the fun of it all, too! I can assure you that one of the primary goals that Maria has with *"My Greek Keto Kitchen"* is for it to be an enjoyable experience that you and your entire family can be involved in, connected to, and appreciated for letting you tap into the Greek side of things.

If you love Greek food and you just didn't know how to make your favourite dishes fit the bill, then this is the book for you. Sometimes you just need a little helping hand from someone who knows a thing or two about Greek cooking along with a passion for the healthy keto lifestyle to show you how you can make this happen in your own home. Maria is your trusted guide to put aside your fears and make this dream a reality. This woman is the real deal and you'll be convinced of that as you start making her delicious recipes from this book.

You made a wise decision getting this book. Now, get in that kitchen and start cooking! Ωπα (or as we call it in the English language, opa)!

-Jimmy Moore, international bestselling author of "*Keto Clarity*"

MY STORY/INTRODUCTION

Growing up Greek meant that I was always surrounded by traditional Greek food. Every occasion and every celebration called for authentic, traditional and delicious Greek cuisine! As a little girl, I have the fondest of memories of my mom spending endless hours in the kitchen preparing food, not only for our family dinners, but for various birthdays, school and community events, as well as for our friends and neighbours. There was never a time when we would have a visitor and food wasn't served. It never happened! It would be an understatement if I were to tell you that my house was like a 24-hour restaurant. I clearly remember my friends and their parents always commenting on how mouth-wateringly fragrant our house was, and how delicious Fay's – that would be my mom, food tasted! You must have heard of "My Big Fat Greek Wedding", right? Do you remember that scene where Toula is going to school with an unusual lunch? Or the scene where the aunt says, "No worries, I make you lamb"? Well, that was me growing up Greek!

Holidays were extra special in our kitchen. We would roll out the traditional cookies, pastries and breads. Some sweet and some savoury but all delightfully delicious! I was always my mom's little helper standing on a chair right by her side, leaning over the table mixing, kneading and forming cookies. She did the very same next to her mother - my grandmother, who taught her so much. I always looked forward to those days when I would get to wear my apron around my little waist and my hair tied up in a bandana. I look back at those moments so fondly and with so much gratitude that I continue the tradition with my two sons.
I was never much of a dieter or stressed about my weight, but there were moments in my life when I compared myself to other girls and wished I were "skinnier". Truth be told, I have had a roller-coaster relationship with my own weight issues. Growing up Greek coupled with my love for food, dieting was never on my radar. As I look back on my childhood, I remember many times when I was unwell. I suffered regularly from bronchitis, was medicated with the typical antibiotics and inhalers and thought these bad colds were just part of growing up. As a young adult I continued to believe that this was normal and just part of life. Fast forward to today…

Hi, my name is Maria Hatzimarkos and I am a Certified Ketogenic Nutritional Coach. I am the owner and founder of *Your KeToRRIfic Journey* that not only offers coaching services but guilt-free *Keto / Low Carb / Paleo* treats as well!

One cannot live on bacon alone, I confess! As I began to realize that living a healthy Keto lifestyle did not require sacrificing variety, flavour and of course our favourite treats, I inspired others to believe that too. We came up with the name *KeToRRific* as a family, with a lot of input from my boys, and for me, it has always been about the journey. And so, *Your KeToRRific Journey* was born and ready to serve up a healthy dish, and yes, we can have our cake and eat it too.

Not long ago I attended a Wellness Conference and the speaker asked us, "Who is your hero, inspiration, or mentor in your life or on your journey?"

Without hesitation or doubt, the person he described is my husband, Tony. He has shown our family some incredible self-love so that it benefit not only himself but his family. His unconditional love, determination and support is unquestionable and to turn his health issues around is a perfect example of his courage and willpower in face of the challenges, and our family was watching. Let me explain.

I will never forget that fateful day in June of 2014 when my husband woke up and announced he was going to start eating a certain way. This was called Keto. He had done his research and had made his decision. If you ask me, I thought he was crazy, "We're Greek and we love food", I screeched!! I also remember my panic when I realized I didn't know how to support him on this new journey. He helped me by sending me lots of information, links and recipes so that I could at least, as a loving partner, prepare Keto-approved meals. Long story short, he reversed his TYPE 2 Diabetes within 3 months and since then has been medication-free and additionally, has stabilized his diagnosis of multiple sclerosis. His doctors declared that "we don't know what you're doing but keep it up!"

It was only when I hurt my back which triggered chronic pain throughout my entire body that I took notice of my own health. With no support from our conventional medical system other than a quick diagnosis of the catch-all "disease" fibromyalgia, I realized I should follow my husband's lead and take charge of my health and wellness plan. With his support and encouragement, I gave Keto a go, and the results are nothing less than incredible!

So, following numerous illnesses affecting my family, it has become not only my passion to share and educate everyone that health should be a number one priority, but my mission!

I share my story with you in the hope that it inspires, motivates, and helps you, your family and your friends take the steps towards making healthier choices using the Keto lifestyle. Without sacrificing flavour and variety, and inspired by my native Greece, I encourage you to explore my keto – and family-approved recipes to help you achieve a healthier you from the inside out.

With much love and support,

Maria

What Is the Ketogenic Diet?

Now for a little science and a little magic, let me explain what the Ketogenic Diet really is. I like to keep it simple and prefer to present it as a lifestyle as the word diet, for many is that "four-letter word" we hate! Alternatively, diets can be a useful solution when considered for temporary use, especially for pre- and post-surgical or other medical procedures. The Keto lifestyle involves eating low carbohydrates, moderate protein and high fats!! Natural healthy fats that is! It is all about providing real food with real ingredients with all the vitamins and minerals the body needs to stay healthy.

Ketosis is the state in which our bodies are burning fat rather than sugar. Adopting the Keto lifestyle means that our bodies will no longer burn sugar (glucose) to use as energy, but instead will burn fat (ketones). Hence, the term Ketogenic.

What many people are unaware of is that insulin is one of the hormones that can affect our health the most. What is insulin, you ask? It is the hormone made by the pancreas and its main function is to lower blood sugar levels when they are too high.

So, every time we consume bread, cookies, crackers, juices and similar foods, our blood sugar levels rise. This signals the pancreas to produce more insulin to restore the blood sugar to healthier levels. When we have excessive amounts of insulin in our body however, it prevents natural fat burning, continues to store fat as a protective mechanism, and increases the glucose or fat in the cells.

Over time, if insulin levels are consistently high, there is a risk of becoming insulin resistant. This means that the pancreas stops responding to blood sugar spikes as it sees it as a new normal. The pancreas stops performing efficiently and the body will then start ignoring what insulin is trying to do -which is to eliminate the glucose in the blood and puts it into our cells instead. Here is some awareness for you – were you aware that insulin resistance is a major cause of health issues? Headaches, skin issues, fatigue, chronic illnesses such as Type 2 Diabetes, inflammation, heart conditions and so much more. Living a healthy Keto lifestyle will help heal insulin resistance symptoms!

The best part about Keto is that we first get healthy. Everyone's wellness goals are different so if your goal is to reverse a diagnosis like fibromyalgia, then, that is what will happen! If your goal is to lose weight, then you will lose weight! Keep in mind however, that weight is typically a symptom of something else like hormones and activity levels. This lifestyle goes much deeper than any other lifestyle can. It can positively affect the health and performance of hormones and overall metabolism.

In summary, what can the Ketogenic lifestyle do?

- Use fat stored in our body as fuel
- Promote weight loss
- Eliminate belly fat
- Improve memory, mental clarity and focus
- Improve mood and balance emotions
- Reduce cravings and hunger
- Invigorate metabolism
- Heal insulin imbalances

You know what they say..."It's never too early nor too late to start making changes that your future self will thank you for". I know this from experience and have the results to prove it. There is an equal amount of great, and not so great information about Keto, so I invite you to reach out to me with your toughest question and turn myths into facts! Share your story with me, because we all have one, and let me help you on your journey. It is time to get real, get informed and start spreading awareness that we can take back control of our health and wellness goals by adopting an effective and easy Keto lifestyle!

Please feel free to follow me and share your KeToRRific Journey with us:
https://www.facebook.com/YourKeToRRificJourney/
https://www.instagram.com/yourketorrificjourney/

What Can I Eat while following this lifestyle and why?

The Keto lifestyle is all about eating real, nutrient-dense food that nourishes the body. Below you will find a pie chart that demonstrates what a Healthy Ketogenic diet looks like. Keep in mind however that everyone's body is different and requires specifically defined percentages of Fat, Protein and Carbohydrates based on several factors. These factors include, activity levels, genetics and current health challenges. Let's shift the relationship we have over the choices we make about food.

To assist you during this journey we have included the percentages and grams of Fat, Protein and Net Carbs (Total Carbs-Fibre=NET CARBS) for each recipe. However, if you are someone who enjoys number crunching and calculating here is the equation in calculating your macro nutrients in the food you consume.

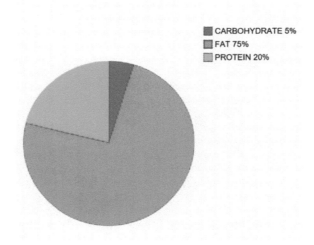

CARBOHYDRATE 5%
FAT 75%
PROTEIN 20%

Fat = 9 calories per gram
Protein = 4 calories per gram
Carbohydrate = 4 calories per gram

(9 x grams of FAT) + (4 x grams of PROTEIN) + (4 x grams of CARBOHYDRATE) = TOTAL CALORIES

Please note that throughout this book when referring to food recommendations, we are speaking about foods that are organic, free-range, pasture-raised, grass-fed and wild-caught.

Why Eat Healthy Proteins & What are Keto-Approved Proteins:

Proteins are essential in our diet for overall good health. They support important functions like repairing and replacing body structures and tissues such as muscles, ligaments, collagen, joints, hair and nails. Proteins definitely provide energy and help with cravings as they help you feel fuller longer. This is why proteins are necessary for controlling blood sugars, and stimulating fat burning hormones. So, a little protein, at every meal and snack will go a long way when it comes to your health and fat burning superpowers!

Here is a list of approved proteins (opt for the fattiest pieces of meat):

- Beef
- Pork (including bacon and sausages, watch out though for hidden sugars such as wheat crumbs and actual sugar)
- Lamb/Goat
- Chicken (opted for dark cut of meets and with skin)
- Duck
- Goose
- Eggs (whole)
- Fish & Sea Food
- Veal
- Turkey
- Organ Meats (liver, heart, kidneys)

Why Eat Healthy Low Carbohydrates & What are Keto-Approved Carbohydrates:

Healthy vegetables on the low carbohydrate scale are full of vitamins such as C, D, E and K. They are low in sugar but high in fiber which helps to block the fat storing hormone, insulin. Furthermore, they are high in potassium which is important in regulating sugar levels, and it assists in eliminating cravings. Potassium is also essential in the controlling and storing of blood sugar. It has unique capabilities to push the sugar into the organs and muscles to perform various functions. Without it, the body will store fat instead and burn the sugar.

An important point to remember is that when insulin levels are low, the body burns fat. When insulin levels are high, the body will store the fat as a protective mechanism and burn the sugar. The goal is to keep insulin levels low to force the body to burn stored fat rather than sugar. Potassium plays a vital role in this process. Equally, potassium helps to balance the sodium ratios. The standard American diet, that includes canned, boxed and overly processed and refined foods, has created a generation of people suffering from water retention due to high sodium and low potassium content in these foods. This is why those following a healthy Keto lifestyle instantly dump a large amount of water weight at the beginning. With proper potassium levels we can achieve the perfect ratios that the cells can tolerate.

Here is a list of approved carbohydrates (opt for the leafy nutrient-rich greens):

- Arugula, Lettuce, Spinach, Swiss Chard, Beet Greens, Kale, Chicory Greens, Watercress
- Sprouts
- Asparagus
- Artichokes
- Broccoli
- Brussels Sprouts
- Cauliflower
- Cabbage
- Cucumbers
- Celery
- Leeks, Onions, Garlic
- Cilantro, Parsley, Dill, Basil, Mint
- Eggplant
- String Beans (Green, Yellow)
- Lemon, Lime
- Mushrooms
- Okra
- Peppers
- Radishes
- Seaweed
- Zucchini

- Tomatoes
- Berries (blackberries, blueberries, strawberries, raspberries)
- Squash

Why Eat Healthy Fats & What are Keto-Approved Fats:

There are endless reasons why healthy fats are essential for our health. A crucial reason is that fats do not affect fat-storing hormones. They are neutral when it comes to insulin levels. Healthy fats keep us satisfied and full all day and provide the body with energy since we are not burning sugar. They are full of many nutrients and fat-soluble vitamins that are essential for good health such as A, E, D, K1 and K2. Generally, we do consume vegetables with these vitamins however, they only contain the precursor of the vitamin, not the converted active form found in fat soluble vitamins. Fat-soluble vitamins are most abundant in foods with a high-fat content and are more easily absorbed into your bloodstream when you eat them with fat. So, don't be afraid to enjoy healthy fats like olive oil and avocado oil with your steamed veggies. It will help your body better absorb all of those wonderful vitamins and minerals that are found in fresh vegetables to help support better hormone balance.

Fat is also needed to protect the cells, the cell walls and to fortify the immune system. We especially need fat to produce hormones, specifically stress and sex hormones like progesterone, estrogen and testosterone. Did you know that out brain is 60% fat and consumes up to 70% of the fats we eat? The brain is perhaps the hungriest of all organs!! Another thing, did you know we also need cholesterol to heal our tissues? Yes, we need cholesterol to heal a cut! What about the fact that we are all born in a state of Ketosis? Bet you didn't know that, did you? Yes indeed.

It is also important to take note of the fact that most of us live in a society where our essential Omega-3 to Omega-6 ratios are off balance. These fatty acids are extremely important to our health and only come from the foods we eat. We need a 1:1 ratio, but unfortunately, many of us have been consuming higher levels of Omega-6 – which can result in inflammation throughout the body, and not enough Omega-3 due, in most part, to low-fat diets. Many of these "low-fat" inflammation-inducing foods include corn oil, seed-based oils and margarine to add flavour and texture once the real fat is removed.

Omega-3 fats include fish, fish oil, walnuts, flax, beef, and chicken.

Omega-6 fats include, sunflower seeds, pumpkin seeds, olive oil, olives, all nuts. Many of these foods even have a combination of both 3 and 6 such as eggs, chicken and beef.

Here is a list of approved healthy fats (full fat, not skim, no low fat anything and watch for hidden sugars in certain products so always read the labels):

- Nuts include Almonds, Pecans, Macadamia Nuts, Brazil Nuts, Walnuts, Pine Nuts, Hazelnuts, Cashews and Pistachios
- Nut Butters include Almond, and cashew,
- Butter
- Avocados
- Avocado Oil
- Coconut Oil
- MCT Oil (Medium Chained Triglycerides)
- Fish Oil
- Flax Oil
- Macadamia Oil
- Almond Oil
- Olive Oil
- Olives
- Cheese from cow (full fat)
- Goat Cheese (such as Greek Feta)
- Cream Cheese (full fat)
- Greek Yogourt (full fat watch out for hidden sugars)
- Sour Cream (full fat watch out for hidden sugars)
- Mayonnaise (full fat)
- Heavy Whipping Cream
- Lard, Tallow, Chicken Fat, Duck Fat, Ghee
- Coconut
- Coconut Cream

- Coconut Milk, Almond Milk, Cashew Milk (unsweetened)
- Seeds include Pumpkin, Sunflower, Sesame, Flax
- Seed Butters: Sunflower, Tahini
- Eggs (whole egg)

As you can see from all of these lists, your food choices are really unlimited! With time you can learn how to put them all together and create incredibly delicious and healthy meals. I truly hope that this cookbook filled with some of our family's favourites inspire and motivate you to start cooking and enjoying healthy Greek meals in your own Keto kitchen. Now, turn the page and let's begin!

Always cheering you on,

Maria

HOW TO USE *"MY GREEK KETO KITCHEN"* FRIENDS

I would like to introduce you to Lemoniá, Elias & Fetoula.

My Greek Keto Kitchen Friends are here to share tips, tricks and more to help you easily create keto-friendly meals. Keep an eye out for them as you go through all of our recipes.

HOW TO USE THE NUT FREE SYMBOL

Nut Free

If you are looking for a nut free option, look for this symbol. This indicates that either the recipe is nut free, or you are given a choice to omit or switch to a nut free option.

HOW TO USE THE DAIRY FREE SYMBOL

Dairy Free

If you are looking for a dairy free option, look for this symbol. This indicates that either the recipe is dairy free, or you are given choice to omit or switch to a dairy free option.

Specialty Items
My Greek Keto Kitchen

The following is a list of specialty ingredients you will find in many Keto/Lowcarb/Paleo recipes when moving away from the Standard American Diet (SAD). As you will see, I steer away from fillers and only use real, simple, and pure ingredients.

- ✓ **Almond Flour**
- ✓ **Coconut Flour**
- ✓ **Psyllium Husk Powder**
- ✓ **Pure Vanilla Extract**
- ✓ **Almond Extract**
- ✓ **Orange Extract**
- ✓ **Baking Powder (gluten free, corn free, aluminum free)**
- ✓ **Coconut Milk (full fat)**
- ✓ **Unsweetened Vanilla Almond Milk**
- ✓ **Unsweetened Shredded Coconut**

Natural Sugar Free Sweeteners

The following is a list of natural sugar-free sweeteners that are made from natural ingredients found in fruits & vegetables. I personally experimented with all of them and found that my preference is the blend of Monk Fruit & Erythritol which measure and taste like sugar. I recommend that you experiment with them yourself, as there are various sweeteners on the market in single form or in blend format. Keep in mind however, that you might have to adjust the amounts as some are concentrated and do not measure or taste like "sugar".

- ✓ **Stevia powder & liquid**
- ✓ **Xylitol**
- ✓ **Erythritol**
- ✓ **Monk Fruit**

Please be aware that Xylitol is toxic to dogs as is chocolate		The recipes that contain "sugar" in this cookbook were created with Monk Fruit & Erythritol Blend

The Greek Keto Pantry
My Greek Keto Kitchen

The following is a list of Greek pantry staple ingredients that you will see being used over and over again in this book, and that are available in most grocery stores. You will find these items in just about every Greek kitchen, however, keep in mind that we are "keto-fying" our Greek family's favourites, hence, it is not an in-depth traditional list. There is nothing better than using simple and pure Greek ingredients in our dishes to bring out those authentic flavours. I have only included basic must-haves that are the foundation of every Greek meal, and as such, this list does not include our healthy proteins and fresh vegetables.

- ✓ **Olives**
- ✓ **Olive Oil**
- ✓ **Lemon**
- ✓ **Garlic**
- ✓ **Nuts such as walnuts and almonds**
- ✓ **Rose water**

Cheeses:
- ✓ **Feta Cheese** *(from sheep's milk or combination of sheep's & goat's milk)*
- ✓ **Kefalograviera / Kefalotyri** *(made from goat's or sheep's milk)*

Herbs & Spices:
- ✓ **Dill**
- ✓ **Parsley**
- ✓ **Mint**
- ✓ **Bay leaves**
- ✓ **Dried oregano**
- ✓ **Sage**
- ✓ **Greek Mountain Tea**
- ✓ **Mastic (Mastiha)**
- ✓ **Cinnamon**

Kali Orexi! Bon appétit! Enjoy Your Meal!

Baking, Cooking & Shopping Tips-Notes
My Greek Keto Kitchen

Depending on where you are in the world, having access to certain ingredients may be a bit challenging. The good news is that with online shopping, we can get our hands on healthier ingredients that may not be available in brick-and-mortar shops due to transportation or other costs. Additionally, more and more merchants are becoming increasingly aware of people's growing needs to obtain clean products. I've created a cheat sheet to help you determine the best ingredients and swaps, when they aren't readily available. I hope this list helps you when you are shopping, planning and preparing in the kitchen.

Don't have powdered low carb sugar? No worries!:
I have a dedicated coffee grinder to powder my monk fruit & erythritol blend.

I personally use monk fruit & erythritol blend:
Feel free to use your choice of approved low carb sugars.
(See page 21)

What to know when choosing a low carb sugar:
Read labels to ensure they are made with pure sources and not mixed with unhealthy sugars such as maltitol, maltodextrin, maltose, dextrose, aspartame to name a few. As these sugar free substitutes may not affect our glucose (blood) levels, they will affect our hormones, and especially spike our insulin. These sugars have a negative effect on our bodies, our overall health including weight-loss. Keep an eye out for actual sugar being added into the blend. Choose a brand with no corn.
I can't say this enough: READ THE LABELS.

What to know when experimenting with low carb sugars:
Read the manufacture's label to verify if you need to adjust the amount. Many are concentrated and do not measure or taste like sugar.

No gluten or yeast:
Keep in mind that when these items are absent from the flours we use, the rise usually seen with traditional recipes will not be as high.

Forming a gluten free dough:

If you are new to a ketogenic lifestyle and have not experimented much with gluten free flours, it might feel a bit overwhelming when attempting to form a ball of dough and rolling it out. Since there is no gluten, we will not get that same consistency nor the gel-like stretch that you will see using traditional flours. It takes some practice and patience at times but do not lose your confidence. I find having wet hands helps work the dough. I always have a small bowl of water next to me to avoid the dough sticking to my hands and it really helps with the rolling. Be careful not to over-add water as the dough will not hold and it will be too sticky. It's about getting that right consistency, not too dry and not too wet. Rolling the dough out in between two sheets of parchment paper is a neat trick that works for me. Practice makes perfect!

Why is my psyllium turning purple?:

Well first of all, why are we adding psyllium?

Psyllium acts like, and replaces the gluten in low-carb flours such as almond and coconut that we use in our recipes. Once water is added, it gives the dough a gel-like elastic texture. As for the colour purple, I personally have not experienced it, however, others have. The good news is that it is only cosmetic, and it does not change the taste or texture of your finished product.

Storing your low-carb flours such as almond, coconut, psyllium:

Once you've opened the packaging of the flour, storing it in an air-tight container in the refrigerator will prolong its shelf life. It can stay fresh for up to 6 months. Warmer temperatures tend to degrade the fats in the nuts, and the oils will turn rancid much quicker if you leave them at room temperature. When you are ready to bake, take the flour out of the refrigerator and use once it has reached room temperature.

Measuring your almond flour and coconut flour:

When it comes to measuring ingredients, especially when baking, I recommend weighing your low-carb flours with a simple kitchen scale. This helps with meeting the accuracy of the recipe and calculating the net carbs. If you do not have a scale at home don't worry. Alternatively, I suggest using the scoop method and "lightly" pack as if you were measuring "brown sugar". Note that the net carbs and other nutritional information may vary depending on brands and measuring methods used. The measured net carbs in *My Greek Keto Kitchen"* were calculated using the kitchen scale method.

When using coconut flour:

Use the kitchen scale measuring method, and then dump into a sifter to avoid any lumps in your batter or dough.

How much salt or pepper is in a pinch or a dash?:

There is much debate around this question and not everyone will agree. It could be anywhere between 1/16 to 1/8 of a teaspoon. And let's be honest, how many of us have a measured 1/16* of a teaspoon in their kitchen drawer? I am also guilty when it comes to measuring, so I just eyeball it. I suggest to measure out 1/8 tsp and divide in half.

When using lemon rinds or zest:

To avoid a bitter aftertaste, only peel or zest the yellow part and not the white part of the lemon. This requires a very sharp knife or peeler for the rind and a very sharp grater for the zest. The trick is to go lightly on the grater while rotating your lemon. If using a knife or peeler and some white remains, simply remove the white part.

Fresh herbs vs spices:

I suggest using the indicated fresh herb or dried spice listed in the recipe. A dried spice can replace fresh herbs but keep in mind that you need much less of a dried spice as the flavours are more concentrated. Measure accordingly.

Greek Feta cheese:

Traditionally, feta cheese is made from sheep's milk, and sometimes a little goat's milk is blended in. It is typically salty and tangy, and usually very rich and creamy, although feta cheese with more goat's milk tends to be crumbly. Unfortunately, this cheese may be hard to come by because of the unpasteurized milk restrictions and high demand in its own country and in the country where you reside. Less often and much less traditionally, cow's milk can be used to make a feta-style cheese. Note that the texture of the feta cheese is less creamy when cow's milk is used instead. Throughout *My Greek Keto Kitchen"*, the Greek feta used, and macro nutrients calculated from, is the variety made from a blend of sheep's and goat's milk.

Greek extra virgin olive oil:

Without trying to be biased, I highly recommend Greek extra virgin olive oil. I choose the "extra virgin" variety for its exceptional quality, aroma, taste and health benefits. The oil comes from the first pressing of the olives and no chemicals or water are added during the processing. Furthermore, purchasing the extra virgin olive oil helps to minimize the chance that your olive oil is blended with refined oils. Extra virgin olive oil goes through extensive checks to be classified as extra virgin olive oil. Other things to look out for is that your olive oil be in a dark bottle to avoid exposure to the light. Exposure to the light can turn your oil rancid. As well, store your olive oil in a dark area of your kitchen or pantry, and do not transfer it into a clear bottle, once again, to avoid light exposure. Although the bottle should be dark, try to look for a golden-green colour to the oil. If you are still hesitating and concerned that you might purchase the wrong olive oil or worse, that it could be refined, consider checking the label and look for the origin of the product and the price. That is, look for key words such as *"made in",* or *"product of".* Words like *"imported from"* or *"packed in"*, does not guarantee that the oil actually originated from olives grown in that country, nor is it any guarantee of quality. And extra virgin olive oil is usually more expensive than olive oil.

Making substitutions:

Keep in mind that if you choose a different type or cut of meat, it may change the macro nutrient ratios I include in the recipe. It is most important to remember that there be some fat, and that you do not switch it for a very lean piece of meat. Otherwise, it would no longer be considered a ketogenic meal. Furthermore, in making substitutions of other ingredients in these recipes, net carbs and other nutritional information may vary depending on brands being used.

MEZEDES-APPETIZERS

KEFTEDAKIA / GREEK MEATBALLS
My Greek Keto Kitchen - Mezedes / Appetizers

Dairy Free   Nut Free

Prep Time: 60 minutes (including rest time in fridge)
Cook Time: 40 minutes
Servings: about 60 meat balls

These Greek meatballs are a step up from your ordinary meat ball! You can enjoy these flavourful delights either grilled, cooked in a skillet or in the oven. The original recipe calls for bread or breadcrumbs and flour to keep them moist, however, we are omitting those ingredients completely to "Ketofy" the recipe and you won't be skimping on flavour. Your taste buds will be yearning for more when you add all of these savoury ingredients together.

Ingredients:

- About 3.3 lbs (1.5 kg) of medium ground beef (no lean meat) or equal parts of medium ground beef, pork and lamb
- 6 spring green onions, finely chopped (include green stems)
- 4 tbs fresh parsley, finely chopped
- 2 tbs fresh mint, finely chopped
- 1 tsp dry oregano
- 4 garlic cloves, finely chopped
- 2 tbs Greek extra virgin olive oil
- 2 tsp pink Himalayan salt or sea salt
- 2-3 pinches of black pepper
- 1 tbs garlic powder
- 3 eggs, beaten
- 1 medium ripe tomato, grated without the skin (about 0.2 lbs – 125 g)

Cooking Method:

1. Add the ground beef to a bowl.
2. Add the finely chopped spring onions, parsley, mint, garlic to the bowl and gently mix together. Add the grated tomato, the beaten eggs, olive oil, herbs and spices, and mix well with a spoon or using your hands.
3. Place the bowl in the refrigerator for about 30 minutes to allow all of the ingredients to blend together.
4. Heat the over to 375F.
5. Remove the bowl from the refrigerator and form into golf-size balls by rolling them between the palm of your hands. Place them evenly spread out on 2 greased baking sheets with parchment paper.
6. Bake for about 40 minutes until slightly browned. Keep an eye on them as oven temperatures may vary slightly. At the half-way point, switch the baking pans from the top to the bottom rack, and the bottom to the top one. This will ensure even baking. If you are using a skillet, heat some avocado oil and fry the meatballs for about 10 minutes on medium heat, turning them frequently.
7. Remove the meatballs from the oven or skillet and place them on a paper towel to drain off any excess fat.
8. Enjoy with your favourite salad, tzatziki or on their own!

MACROS: (per meatball)
Calories: 66.3
Fat: 4.8 g / 65.9%
Protein: 5.1 g / 31.7%
Net Carbs: 0.33 g / 2.4%

At times when baking in the oven, a layer of fat may accumulate around the meatballs due to excess liquid or fat. Just remove by blotting them on a paper towel and enjoy once cooled.

MELITZANOSALATA / EGGPLANT SALAD (DIP)
My Greek Keto Kitchen - Mezedes / Appetizers

Dairy Free

Nut Free

Prep Time: 1 hour 20 minutes (including cool down period)
Cook Time: 40 minutes
Servings: 8

Even though its name implies salad, it is typically eaten as a dip. If you enjoy dips with your favourite vegetables, bread or crackers, you will definitely add this one to your list. Be adventurous and add diced tomatoes, capers or even walnuts to add extra texture and level of flavour.

Ingredients:

- About 4.4 lbs (2 kg) of eggplants washed and top ends trimmed (about 3 medium sized eggplants) *See NOTE BELOW
- 1/4 cup (60 ml) of Greek extra virgin olive oil
- 2 tbs of apple cider vinegar
- 1/2 tsp of pink Himalayan salt or sea salt
- 2-3 pinches of black pepper
- 3 garlic cloves
- 2 spring onions
- 1/2 bunch of parsley

Cooking Method:

1. Preheat oven at 375F.
2. Pierce the eggplants all over with a fork.
3. Place them on a baking sheet and cook for about 40 minutes or until softened (pierce with a fork to see if ready)
4. Make a slit across the length of the eggplants to let the steam escape and set aside to cool for about 10 minutes.

5. Use a spoon to scoop out the flesh, place in a colander and discard the skin and most of the seeds.

6. Using a large wooden spoon or your hands, press against the eggplant flesh while in a colander to remove excess liquid as it is bitter and may spoil the flavour. Discard the skin and the seeds. Leave the eggplant in the colander for about 1 hour to ensure all the liquid has drained.

7. Remove the eggplant and roughly chop or pulse in a food processor. Place aside in a bowl.

8. In a food processor, add the olive oil, garlic, apple cider vinegar, salt and pepper and pulse until the garlic is completely broken down. You can than add the parsley and continue to pulse.

9. Finely chop the green onions.

10. Add the chopped onions and the garlic-oil to the bowl of eggplant and stir well.

11. Add salt to taste and end with a drizzle of olive oil and apple cider vinegar.

MACROS: (about 265 g per serving)
Calories: 92.9
Fat: 7 g / 67.2%
Protein: 0.9 g / 2.3%
Net Carbs: 5.56 g / 30.5%

After baking the eggplants and removing the skin and most seeds you should have approximately 1.5 lbs (670 g) of eggplant.

SKORDALIA / GARLIC MASH
My Greek Keto Kitchen - Mezedes / Appetizers

Dairy Free   Nut Free

Prep Time: 20 minutes
Cook Time: 15 minutes
Servings: 4

This popular Greek side-dish is traditionally made with potatoes or bread. Some areas of Greece add walnuts to add thickness and texture by grinding a handful and sprinkling it on top. Enjoy this mash with fish, meat or vegetables such as eggplants, zucchini or wild greens. This dish can also be served as a dip.

Ingredients:

- About 1.1 lbs (500 g) of cauliflower (you can use frozen)
- 1/2 cup (118 ml) of Greek extra virgin olive oil
- 2 tbs of apple cider vinegar
- 1/2 tsp of pink Himalayan salt or sea salt
- 2-3 pinches of black pepper
- 2 garlic cloves

Cooking Method:

1. Fill a pot with water and place on high heat.
2. Add 1 teaspoon of salt and bring to a boil.
3. Chop the cauliflower into small pieces and add them to the pot of boiling water or place directly from frozen.
4. Boil for about 10-15 minutes until they are soft. Note: the boiling time will depend on the size of the cauliflower pieces.
5. In a food processor, add the olive oil, garlic, apple cider vinegar, salt and pepper. Beat until the garlic completely breaks down.

6. Pierce the cauliflower with a fork to check for doneness, drain and set aside for 10 minutes to allow the steam to completely evaporate. This is an important step as you do not want it to be watery as it will affect the outcome.
7. Once cooled, immediately transfer the cauliflower and mash them with a potato masher or a fork.
8. Add the garlic and oil mixture and incorporate well.
9. Season to taste with salt and pepper.

MACROS: (about 135 g per serving)
Calories: 228.6
Fat: 22.8 g / 89.5%
Protein: 2.1 g / 2.3%
Net Carbs: 1.74 g / 8.2%

Keep in mind that with time, the garlic flavour becomes stronger and the puree thickens.

Optional: Sprinkle with chopped fresh green onions, parsley, olive oil and/or walnuts (not calculated in macros)

TIROKAFTERI, KOPANISTI, HTIPITI / SPICY CHEESE DIPS
My Greek Keto Kitchen - Mezedes / Appetizers

Nut Free

All three of these dips are derived from the Greek word "tiri, which means cheese, "kafteri" - spicy, and "kopanisti"/"htipiti" - to be beaten. These salty, creamy with just-enough-heat dips can be found at any home gathering or restaurant and will please any crowd! Enjoy it with cucumber slices, celery, Keto/Low Carb/ Paleo pita or bread, or as side dip for meat. So, give them a try and see which becomes your favourite!

TIROKAFTERI / SPICY GREEK FETA DIP

Prep Time: 20 minutes
Servings: 4

Ingredients:

- 8 oz (226.8 g) Greek feta cheese
- 3 tbs of Greek extra virgin olive oil
- 3 tbs heavy cream
- 1 tbs of apple cider vinegar
- 2 garlic cloves
- 2 spring green onions, including the green stems - washed and trimmed
- 1/2 tbs dried oregano
- 1 tbs chili flakes (for a less spicy dish, use only ½ tbs)

Cooking Method:

1. In a food processor add, olive oil, garlic, onions, cream, chili flakes and puree.
2. Add Greek feta cheese, apple cider vinegar, oregano and blend until smooth.
3. Enjoy immediately or place in the refrigerator until ready to consume.

HTIPITI / GREEK FETA and ROASTED RED PEPPER DIP

Prep Time: 20 minutes
Cook Time: 35 minutes (including cool downtime)
Servings: 4

Ingredients:

- 8 oz (226.8 g) Greek feta cheese
- 2 tbs of Greek extra virgin olive oil
- 1 large roasted red pepper (about 6 oz -170 g cooked)
- 1 tbs of apple cider vinegar
- 2 garlic cloves
- 2 spring green onions including green stems - washed and trimmed
- 1 1/2 tsp dried oregano
- 1/2 tbs chili flakes (or to taste)

Cooking Method:

1. Pre heat oven to 370F.
2. Place red pepper on a baking sheet and place in the oven. Bake for about 20 minutes or until tender.
3. Place cooked red pepper in a bowl and cover tightly with cellophane wrap for about 15 minutes. Gently shake the bowl. This trick of steaming the peppers and shaking helps remove the skin from the pepper. Peel off the skin from the peppers. Allow to cool.
4. In a food processor add, olive oil, garlic, green onions, red pepper, chili flakes and puree.
5. Add Greek feta cheese, apple cider vinegar, oregano and blend until smooth.
   Enjoy immediately or place in the refrigerator until ready to consume.

KOPANISTI / GREEK FETA CHEESE and MINT DIP

Prep Time: 20 minutes
Servings: 4

Ingredients:

- 8 oz (226.8 g) Greek feta cheese
- 4 tbs of Greek extra virgin olive oil
- 2 tbs of fresh lemon juice
- 2 garlic cloves
- 10-12 leaves of fresh mint
- 1/2 tsp chili flakes (or to taste)

Cooking Method:

1. In a food processor add, olive oil, garlic, lemon juice, fresh mint and chili flakes and puree.
2. Add Greek feta cheese and blend until smooth.
3. Enjoy immediately or place in refrigerator until ready to consume.

MACROS for Tirokafteri: (about 80 g per serving)
Calories: 306.7
Fat: 27.1 g / 82.8%
Protein: 9.8 g / 13.8%
Net Carbs: 1.79 g / 3.4%

MACROS for Htipiti: (about 100 g per serving)
Calories: 245.9
Fat: 20.1 g / 77.6%
Protein: 10 g / 17.2%
Net Carbs: 2.81 g / 5.2%

MACROS for Kopanisti: (about 65 g per serving)
Calories: 295.6
Fat: 26.8 g / 84.9%
Protein: 9.6 g / 14%
Net Carbs: 0.97 g / 1.1%

From Top to Bottom:
TIROKAFTERI / SPICY GREEK FETA DIP
KOPANISTI / GREEKFETA CHEESE and MINT DIP
HTIPITI / GREEK FETA and ROASTED RED PEPPER DIP

DOMATOKEFTEDES / TOMATO FRITTERS (KEFTEDES)
My Greek Keto Kitchen - Mezedes / Appetizers

Prep Time: 60 minutes (including refrigeration time)
Cook Time: 30-40 minutes
Servings: approx. 26 fritters

There is something about these Greek fritters that reminds me of my grandmother. She was the Queen of Fritters! So, in my effort in keeping with tradition, I am so pleased that I was able to omit the white flour and breadcrumbs, and managed to keep the amazing taste.

Ingredients:

- 4 medium tomatoes (I used fresh Roma tomatoes since they have less seeds) - approx. 1.5 lbs (700 g)
- 1 small onion finely chopped – approx. 0.2 lbs (95 g)
- 5 oz (150 g) of Greek feta cheese
- 1 cup (112 g) almond flour
- 4 tbs coconut flour
- 10-12 mint leaves finely chopped - approx. 1 tbs.
- 1/2 cup (30 g) flat leaf parsley, finely chopped
- 1 tsp dried oregano
- 1 tbs garlic powder
- 1/2 tsp pink Himalayan salt or sea salt
- 4-5 dashes of black pepper
- 2 large eggs, beaten

Cooking Method:

1. Pre-heat oven to 370F
2. Finely chop the tomatoes, onion and fine herbs and place them all in a large bowl.
3. Using a fork, crumble the Greek feta in a small bowl and add salt, pepper, garlic powder, oregano and the beaten eggs. Mix well in large bowl.

4. Add the almond flour and mix until well combined. Place in the refrigerator for approx. 20 minutes to allow the flour and the rest of the ingredients to incorporate well.
5. In the meantime, prepare 2 baking sheets with parchment paper.
6. Remove the bowl from the refrigerator and add the coconut flour, one tablespoon at a time. Allow to sit for approx. 5 minutes for the flour to absorb all the liquid and flavours.
7. Using a regular tablespoon, scoop up the batter and drop onto prepared baking sheets.
8. Bake for approximately 30 minutes or until slightly golden-brown. Alternate the baking sheets half-way through to ensure even baking.
9. Enjoy warm or at room temperature!

MACROS: (per fritter)
Calories: 63.5
Fat: 4.2 g / 62.2%
Protein: 2.9 g / 18.1%
Net Carbs: 1.83 g / 19.7%

TZATZIKI / CUCUMBER, GARLIC & YOGURT GREEK DIP

My Greek Keto Kitchen - Mezedes / Appetizers

Nut Free

Prep Time: 30 minutes
Servings: 8-12 servings

This creamy and refreshing sauce is the best compliment to any Greek Mediterranean dish! Greek style yogurt can easily be found in any Greek or Middle Eastern Market. However, be cautions of hidden sugars and look for the authentic strained version which has more fat and very little carbohydrates. I used a version that contained both cow and goat milk.

Ingredients:

- 2 cups (about 500 ml) strained yogurt
- 1/2 English cucumber grated – approx. 3/4 cup (170 g) of pulp after it is drained of all liquid
- 2 tbs of Greek extra virgin olive oil
- 1 tbs of apple cider vinegar
- Pink Himalayan salt or sea salt, to taste
- Black pepper, to taste
- 3 garlic cloves, minced or grated

Cooking Method:

1. Grate cucumber and place in a colander to allow the liquid to drain. A trick you can use to help release the liquid is to cover the pulp with a heavy platter or cast-iron pan and let it sit. Alternatively, using your hands or the back of a spoon to press against the pulp will require some elbow grease, but equally effective.
2. Grate or finely chop the garlic.

3. Place strained yogurt, garlic, apple cider vinegar, olive oil and strained cucumber into a bowl and mix well.
4. Add salt and pepper to taste and mix well once again.
5. Place the bowl in the refrigerator until ready to enjoy.

MACROS: (about 55 g per serving)
Calories: 86.1
Fat: 6.5 g / 67.5%
Protein: 4.3 g / 19.6%
Net Carbs: 2.66 g / 13%

KOLOKITHOKEFTEDES / ZUCCHINI FRITTERS (KEFTEDES)
My Greek Keto Kitchen - Mezedes / Appetizers

Prep Time: 60 minutes (including refrigeration time)
Cook Time: 30 minutes
Servings: about 32 fritters

These Greek fritters are a mouthful, not only to pronounce (koh-loh-kee-thoh-kef-TEH-thes), *but, of flavour as well! These are one of our family's favourite mezedes and make a delicious side dish to any meal.*

Ingredients:

- 4 or 5 zucchini's – approx. 2.3 lbs (1 kg) (reduced to 1.3 lbs - 600 g after straining)
- 6 green onions - including green stems, finely chopped
- 10 oz (283.5 g) of Greek feta cheese
- 1 1/4 cup (140 g) almond flour
- 4 tbs coconut flour
- 5 tbs fresh dill, finely chopped
- 3 tbs fresh mint - leaves only, finely chopped
- 1 tbs garlic powder
- 1/2 tsp pink Himalayan salt or sea salt
- 1/4 tsp black pepper
- 4 large eggs, beaten

Cooking Method:

1. Pre-heat the oven to 370F
2. Grate zucchini and place in a colander, with a little salt, to allow the liquid to drain. A trick you can apply to help release the liquid is to cover the pulp with a heavy platter or cast-iron pan and let it sit. Alternatively, using your hands or the back of a spoon to press against the pulp will require some elbow grease, but equally effective. The key to the success of these fritters is that they are as dry as possible, which not only adds to the flavor, but helps maintain their shape while baking.
3. Finely chop the green onions and herbs and place them all in a large bowl.

4. Using a fork, crumble the Greek feta and place it in the same bowl. Add pepper, garlic powder and the beaten egg. Mix together well.
5. Add the well-strained zucchini to the bowl.
6. Add the almond flour and mix until well combined. Place in the refrigerator for about 20 minutes to allow the flour and the rest of the ingredients to incorporate well.
7. In the meantime, prepare 2 baking sheets with parchment paper.
8. Remove the bowl from the refrigerator and add the coconut flour, one tablespoon at a time. Allow to sit for approx. 5 minutes for the flour to absorb all the liquid and flavours.
9. Using a regular tablespoon, scoop up the batter and drop onto prepared baking sheets.
10. Bake for approximately 30 minutes or until slightly golden-brown. Alternate the baking sheets half-way through to ensure even baking.
11. Enjoy warm or at room temperature!

MACROS: (per fritter)
Calories: 72.7
Fat: 5.2 g / 67.1%
Protein: 3.7 g / 20.5%
Net Carbs: 1.16 g / 12.4%

SALADS-VEGETABLES

SALATA KOUNOUPIDIOU / CAULIFLOWER SALAD

My Greek Keto Kitchen: Salad / Vegetable Dishes

Dairy Free

Nut Free

Prep Time: 30 minutes (including cool down time)
Cook Time: 15 minutes
Servings: 4

This refreshing and simple salad could be enjoyed as a side dish or a meal all on its own. Cauliflower is so versatile, and not to mention good for you! It is naturally high in fibre and B-vitamins, an antioxidant, contains cancer preventing phytonutrients, and more!

Ingredients:

- 1 whole large cauliflower head about 1.3 lbs (600 g), washed and trimmed *(do not cut into pieces)*
- 1 whole lemon, yielding about 2 tbs fresh lemon juice
- ¼ cup (60 ml) Greek extra virgin olive oil
- 2 to 3 cloves of fresh garlic, finely chopped or grated
- 1/2 tsp pink Himalayan salt or sea salt (or salt to taste) and a couple more pinches for salted water
- 2 to 3 pinches of black pepper
- 1/4 tsp dried oregano

Cooking Method:

1. Place whole cauliflower head in a large pot with water and a few pinches of salt.
2. Bring water to a boil, then lower to medium heat and simmer for about 10 minutes, or until cauliflower is tender.
3. When you can easily pierce the cauliflower, drain and set aside to cool down and to allow all the steam to evaporate. **This is an important step to release as much water as possible to avoid a mushy consistency.*

4. In the meantime, mix the ingredients for the dressing: lemon juice, olive oil, garlic, salt, pepper and oregano, and let the flavours emulsify to enhance the flavours. Taste dressing and adjust seasoning to taste with more salt, pepper and lemon juice.
5. Once the cauliflower has cooled, place it in a bowl, pour the dressing over the cooked cauliflower head.

MACROS: (About 150 g per serving)
Calories: 148.5
Fat: 13 g / 78.8%
Protein: 2.7 g / 4.6%
Net Carbs: 3.6 g / 16.7%

PRASINI SALATA FASOLION / GREEN BEAN SALAD
My Greek Keto Kitchen: Salad / Vegetable Dishes

Dairy Free   Nut Free

Prep Time: 30 minutes
Cook Time: 15 minutes
Servings: 4

Green beans are healthy and delicious any way they are prepared. In the summer months, enjoy them on a hot day when you want a quick and hearty meal or side dish cold in a salad, or warm with melting butter and herbs. This refreshing and simple salad can certainly be enjoyed all year long. Feel free to add some crumbled feta cheese to complete the flavours. NB: the macro nutrients do not include the feta cheese.

Ingredients:

- 1.1 lbs (500 g) green beans, washed and trimmed
- 1 whole lemon (yielding 2 tbs fresh lemon juice) * *add more to taste if you like lemon flavouring*
- ¼ cup (60 ml) Greek extra virgin olive oil
- 2 to 3 cloves of fresh garlic, finely chopped or grated
- ½ tsp pink Himalayan salt or sea salt for the vinaigrette * *add more to taste*
- ½ tsp pink Himalayan salt or sea salt for water
- 2 to 3 pinches of black pepper
- ¼ tsp dried oregano

Cooking Method:

1. Place cleaned and trimmed beans in a large pot with salted water
2. Bring water to a boil, then lower to medium heat and simmer for about 10 minutes or until beans are tender or easily pierced with a fork. *I prefer them with a little snap, so I don't let them boil too long.*

3. When the green beans are ready, drain and set aside to cool down and to allow all of the steam to evaporate. *This is an important step to release as much water as possible to avoid a mushy consistency.*
4. In the meanwhile, mix the ingredients for the dressing: lemon juice, olive oil, garlic, salt, pepper and oregano, and let the flavours emulsify to enhance the flavours. Taste the dressing and adjust seasoning to taste with salt, pepper and lemon juice.
5. Once the green beans have cooled, place them in a bowl, pour in the dressing and mix gently.

MACROS: (about 135 g per serving)
Calories: 151.4
Fat: 12.6 g / 74.9%
Protein: 2 g / 3.3%
Net Carbs: 5.39 g / 21.8%

ELLINIKI SALATA ME PIPERIES STI SKARA / GREEK GRILLED PEPPER SALAD

My Greek Keto Kitchen: Salad / Vegetable Dishes

Dairy Free

Nut Free

Prep Time: 20 minutes
Cook Time: 35 minutes (including the cool down time)
Servings: 8

This Greek side dish is always a crowd pleaser. There is nothing like the sweet and savoury taste of roasted peppers! You can either grill them on an outdoor or indoor grill or roast them in the oven. The marriage of roasted peppers and the garlicky dressing is a union that is simply irresistible and a favourite keto side dish on our kitchen table.

Ingredients:

- 3 large red peppers (about 1.7 lbs - 800 g) *feel free to use green or yellow peppers.
- 1 tbs apple cider vinegar
- 1 tbs Greek extra virgin olive oil and a little more for final drizzle
- 1/2 tsp garlic powder
- 1/4 tsp pink Himalayan salt or sea salt
- 2 dashes of black pepper
- 1/4 tsp dried oregano
- 2 oz (60 g) of Greek feta cheese

Cooking Method:

1. Pre-heat grill to medium high.
2. Wash and trim peppers. Slice in half, and then in half again trimming the veins and removing the seeds. You should have 4 wedges per pepper.
3. In a small bowl, whisk together olive oil, salt, pepper and garlic powder.
4. Pour mixture over the peppers and coat well.

5. Grill peppers until soft and slightly charred on both sides for about 20 minutes. If baking in the oven, line a baking pan with parchment paper and spread peppers evenly. Bake for about 30 minutes at 370F (time will vary for each oven so watch regularly for burning)
6. Place them in a bowl and cover tightly with cellophane for about 15 minutes. Gently shake the bowl. This trick allows the peppers to steam, and shaking them, helps to easily remove the charred skin.
7. Once they have cooled and are easy to handle, peel off the skin and place in a bowl.
8. Once cleaned, drizzle the peppers with a little more olive oil, add oregano, apple cider vinegar. If adding, include the crumbled or diced Feta Cheese.
9. Salt and pepper to desired taste. Enjoy!

MACROS: (about 100 g per serving)
Calories: 81.2
Fat: 5.3 g / 60.6%
Protein: 2.2 g / 9.5%
Net Carbs: 5.47 g / 29.8%

Macros are calculated using Greek Feta Cheese. This is optional, you may remove cheese if avoiding dairy.

ELLINIKI SALATA ME KRITHARAKI / GREEK ORZO SALAD (FAUX)

My Greek Keto Kitchen: Salad / Vegetable Dishes

Dairy Free

Nut Free

Prep Time: 2h 20 minutes (including the absorption of liquid)
Servings: 12

Orzo Salad has always been one of my favourite dishes, so I just had to make a keto-friendly version. There is something about this recipe that says, "Welcome Spring!": maybe because of the bright and vibrant colours! This refreshing and simple salad could be enjoyed all year long, in every season. It can be enjoyed all by itself or as a side dish, so the possibilities are endless. Keep in mind that this recipe feeds a crowd at 12 servings. This salad also tastes even better as a leftover, if there is any! You can easily half the recipe if necessary.

Ingredients:

- 1.5 lbs (700 g) raw cauliflower florets (yields about 6 cups of riced cauliflower)
- 1/3 cup (75 ml) fresh lemon juice
- 1/2 cup (118 ml) Greek extra virgin olive oil
- 5 cloves of fresh garlic, finely chopped or grated, or 2 tsp garlic powder
- 1tsp pink Himalayan salt or sea salt
- ¼ tsp black pepper
- 1 medium red onion diced (about ½ cup – 97 g)
- 9 oz (250 g) crumbled Greek Feta cheese
- 5 cups (about 1.250 g) diced tomatoes (Italian or cherry tomatoes)
- 3 tbs fresh coriander, chopped
- 2 cups (120 g) frizzy parsley, chopped
- 2 cups (about 453 g) sliced kalamata olives

Cooking Method:

1. Wash cauliflower and cut into florets. Place florets into a food processor (in batches and not all at once) and *SLOWLY PULSE* until cauliflower resembles rice. *NOTE: Be cautious not to over-pulse the cauliflower to avoid turning it into a mash. It happened to me a few times and I learned my lesson to not rush this step and to use the PULSE function and not the chop/blend.*
2. Place cauliflower rice on a tea towel or paper towel for a couple of hours to absorb moisture.
3. Place riced cauliflower in a big salad bowl.
4. Dice tomatoes and onion either in food processor or with a knife and add to the salad bowl.
5. Chop coriander and parsley either in a food processor or with a knife and add to the salad bowl.
6. Crumble the Greek Feta cheese and add to the salad bowl.
7. Slice Kalamata olives, or if purchased pre-sliced, add to the salad bowl.
8. For the salad dressing, add the remainder of the ingredients; lemon juice, olive oil, garlic, salt, pepper to a small bowl, mix well, and let the flavours emulsify to enhance the flavours.
9. Pour the dressing over the vegetables and mix well. Taste the salad and adjust the seasonings to taste with more salt, pepper and lemon juice.

MACROS: (about 250 g per serving)
Calories: 301
Fat: 24.7 g / 73.4%
Protein: 6 g / 7.5%
Net Carbs: 11.29 g / 19.1%

Macros are calculated using Greek Feta Cheese. This is optional, you may remove cheese if avoiding dairy.

ELLINIKI SALATA ME KOLOKYTHAKIA STI SKARA / GREEK GRILLED ZUCCHINI SALAD

My Greek Keto Kitchen: Salad / Vegetable Dishes

Dairy Free   Nut Free

Prep Time: 20 minutes
Cook Time: 20 minutes
Servings: 4

This salad is simple and delicious and is a great way to add veggies to your meals! This salad makes a great side dish or a complete meal and can be made on either an outdoor or indoor grill or roasted in the oven.

Ingredients:

- 6 medium to large zucchinis (about 1 kg or a little over 2 lbs)
- 1 tbs apple cider vinegar
- 2 tbs Greek extra virgin olive oil and a little more for drizzling
- 1 tsp garlic powder
- 1/2 tsp pink Himalayan salt or sea salt
- 2 to 3 dashes of black pepper
- ¼ tsp dried oregano
- 4 oz (110 g) of Greek Feta cheese

Cooking Method:

1. Pre-heat grill to medium high.
2. Wash and trim zucchini. Slice in half and then lengthwise into ¼-inch slices.
3. In a small bowl, whisk together olive oil, salt, pepper and garlic powder. Pour mixture over the sliced zucchini and coat well.
4. Grill zucchini until soft and slightly charred on both sides, about 15 minutes turning halfway. If baking in the oven, line a baking pan with parchment paper and spread zucchini evenly. Bake for about 30 minutes at 370F *(* time can vary, so keep an eye on them to prevent burning).*

5. Once slightly cooled, drizzle with a little more olive oil, add oregano, apple cider vinegar and crumbled or diced Feta cheese.
6. Salt and pepper to desired taste. Enjoy!

MACROS: (about 280 g per serving)
Calories: 204.1
Fat: 16.3 g / 73.7%
Protein: 7.6 g / 13.3%
Net Carbs: 4.67 g / 13%

Macros are calculated using Greek Feta Cheese. This is optional, you may remove cheese if avoiding dairy.

HORIATIKI SALATA / GREEK SALAD
My Greek Keto Kitchen: Salad / Vegetable Dishes

Dairy Free   Nut Free

Prep Time: 20 minutes
Servings: 4

*This refreshing and simple salad could be enjoyed as a side dish or a meal on its own. It is a staple in Greek homes and is found in many restaurants worldwide whether they are Greek or not. The word **Horiatiki** actually means **village** and this "village salad" has many variations and the traditional version does not include lettuce, however, for the love of greens and the importance of them, I included them in this recipe. Feel free to omit.*

Ingredients:

- 5 large tomatoes (about 1.2 lbs - 550 g)
- 1 bell pepper (green, red, yellow or orange) (about 0.4 lbs -164 g)
- 1 English cucumber (about 0.7 lbs - 300 g)
- 1 small red onion (about 0.2 lbs – 70 g)
- 1 head of romaine lettuce (about 4 cups - 224 g) (you may omit)
- 8 oz (227 g) of authentic Greek Feta cheese
- A handful of Kalamata olives (about 15)
- 1 whole lemon (yielding about 2 tbs fresh lemon juice) or apple cider vinegar
  (I prefer apple cider vinegar)
- 1/4 cup (60 ml) Greek extra virgin olive oil (plus 1 tbs for drizzling over feta cheese)
- 1/2 tsp pink Himalayan salt or sea salt (or to taste)
- 2 to 3 pinches of black pepper
- 1/4 tsp dried oregano (plus a little extra to sprinkle over feta cheese)

Cooking Method:

1. Wash all vegetables thoroughly and let dry.
2. Cut tomatoes into wedges.
3. Cut cucumber, onion, pepper and lettuce into slices.
4. Place everything in a bowl including the olives and mix the remainder of the ingredients in a small separate bowl: lemon juice/apple cider vinegar, olive oil, salt, pepper and oregano, and let the flavours emulsify to enhance the flavours. Taste dressing and adjust seasoning as needed with more salt, pepper and lemon juice or apple cider vinegar. Be careful to not over-salt as olives and feta are salty ingredients.
5. Pour dressing over the salad and toss all the ingredients together. You can either crumble the piece of feta on top or leave as a slice. Drizzle a little more extra virgin olive oil and a little oregano on the feta.

MACROS: (about 400 g per serving)
Calories: 377.5
Fat: 31.7 g / 74.5%
Protein: 12.7 g / 12.5%
Net Carbs: 8.76 g / 13%

Macros are calculated using Greek Feta Cheese. This is optional, you may remove cheese if avoiding dairy.

RADIKIA (HORTA) SALATA / DANDELION (GREENS) SALAD
My Greek Keto Kitchen: Salad / Vegetable Dishes

Dairy Free

Nut Free

Prep Time: 20 minutes
Cook Time: 20 minutes
Servings: 4

Greens (horta) are a traditional staple in Greek cuisine either as a side dish or a main dish, and can be enjoyed warm or cold. Feel free to use any greens besides dandelions such as spinach, kale, beet tops, collard greens, swiss chard and amaranth. Greens are full of vitamins, minerals and fibre. As a side note, when straining the dandelions, save the water and enjoy as a dandelion tea for additional health benefits.

Ingredients:

- 2 bunches of dandelions washed and trimmed. (yields about 6 cups – 630 g) of cooked dandelions)
- 1 whole lemon (yields 1/4 cup – 60 ml fresh lemon juice) * *you may add more if you like lemon flavouring*
- ¼ cup (60 ml) Greek extra virgin olive oil.
- 2 to 3 cloves fresh garlic, finely chopped or grated.
- ½ tsp pink Himalayan salt or sea salt (or salt to taste) and a few more pinches for salting water
- 2 to 3 pinches of black pepper

Cooking Method:

1. Place cleaned and trimmed greens in a large pot with water and a few pinches of salt.
2. Bring water to a boil, then lower to medium heat and simmer for about 15 to 20 minutes or until greens are tender when pierced with a fork. *I prefer my greens with a little snap, so I don't let them boil too long.*

3. When your greens are ready, drain and set aside to cool. *I enjoy them room temperature, however, this is a preference.*
4. In the meanwhile, mix the remainder of the dressing ingredients: lemon juice, olive oil, garlic, salt and pepper, and let the flavours emulsify, to enhance the flavours. Taste the dressing and adjust seasoning to taste with salt, pepper and lemon juice.
5. Once the greens have cooled, place them in a bowl, pour in the dressing and mix gently.

MACROS: (about 170 g per serving)
Calories: 178.4
Fat: 14.5 g / 72.9%
Protein: 3.3 g / 4.6%
Net Carbs: 6.77 g / 22.5%

TRADITIONAL DISHES

BIFTEKIA / GREEK HAMBURGERS
My Greek Keto Kitchen: Traditional Dishes

Dairy Free

Nut Free

Prep Time: 60 minutes (including refrigeration time)
Cook Time: 15 minutes
Servings: about 15 patties

These are not your ordinary hamburgers! You will never find a plain piece of meat on a Greek table! Lamb, beef, chicken and fish are always treated to a mix of herbs and spices authentic to Greek cuisine that create that unique flavour. Ground beef is by no means an exception! Enjoy these nutritious and flavourful patties grilled on a barbeque, seared in a skillet, or baked in the oven. As the original recipe calls for bread or breadcrumbs, we are omitting them to ensure a purely "Ketofied" burger. We could, however, add almond flour, but I don't see why we would add extra carbs when they are delicious just as they are.

Ingredients:

- About 4 lbs (2 kg) of medium ground beef (no lean meat)
- 2 medium sized onions, finely chopped (about 1 1/2 cups -188 g)
- 3 tbs fresh parsley, finely chopped
- 3 tbs fresh mint, finely chopped
- 2 tsp dried oregano
- 5 garlic cloves, finely chopped
- 2 tbs Greek extra virgin olive oil
- 2 tsp pink Himalayan salt or sea salt
- 2-3 pinches of black pepper
- 1 tbs garlic powder
- 2 large eggs, beaten

Cooking Method:

1. Place beef in a bowl.
2. Add the finely chopped onions, parsley, mint. Combine and then add the rest of the ingredients and mix until they are all incorporated. Feel free to mix or knead with your hands.
3. Place bowl in the refrigerator for about 30 minutes to allow all the flavours to emulsify.
4. Form the flavoured beef into patties by rolling into a baseball-sized ball, and then simply flatten it with your hand. Keep in mind, these are smaller than your average hamburger.
5. Heat your grill to medium/high. Once heated, grill patties for about 5 minutes on each side. Keep an eye on them as each grill is different. If broiling in the oven set temperature to 375F. They are ready once cooked through.
6. Enjoy with your choice of a salad, with tzatziki or on their own!

MACROS: (per patties)
Calories: 338.2
Fat: 24 g / 65.4%
Protein: 26.5 g / 32%
Net Carbs: 1.96 g / 2.7%

SOUVLAKI / GREEK PORK ON A SKEWER

My Greek Keto Kitchen: Traditional Dishes

Dairy Free

Nut Free

Prep Time: 1 hour (including refrigeration)
Cook Time: approximately 40 minutes
Servings: 14 skewers (based on 30 cm / 12 in metal skewers which I used)

*This Greek specialty is known world-wide and is made of pork tenderloin and a mix of Greek spices. Traditionally, it is made with pork, however, chicken, beef or lamb are often used, and appear on the menu of your favourite Greek restaurants. You may cook the meat either in an oven or on a stove-to grilling pan, but our favourite way, is on an outside grill or BBQ. There are various ways to enjoy souvlaki which is typically served on the skewer with aside of Greek salad, with a side of rice or potatoes, or wrapped in Greek pita bread with all the trimmings such as onions, tomatoes and tzatziki. You can also enjoy a souvlaki stick on its own with a generous scoop of tzatziki. To keep things "Ketofied", try it with one of your favourite KeToRRific Salads or Vegetable Dish **(page 50 for recipes)**, and our delicious Tzatziki **(page 44 for recipe)** and your choice of Greek Pita **(page 133 for recipe).** The possibilities are endless!*
P.S. Thank you to my husband for sharing his recipe with us.

Ingredients:

- About 7 lbs (3 kg) of pork tenderloin, trimmed of silvery connective tissue, but leave the fat
- 2 tsp dry oregano
- 3 tbs Greek extra virgin olive oil
- juice from a whole fresh lemon, (about 1/4 cup - 60 ml)
- 2 tsp pink Himalayan salt or sea salt
- 2 - 3 pinches of black pepper
- 1 tbs garlic powder
- Bamboo skewers or metal (I used 14 metal skewers)

Cooking Method:

1. If using bamboo skewers, allow them to soak in a shallow pan with water for a couple of hours. This trick eliminates the bamboo skewers from splitting and burning or getting a wood sliver in your meat.
2. Cut pork into about 1 1/2-inch pieces and place in a big bowl.
3. In a small bowl, add the ingredients to build the marinade, and mix well. Pour the marinade mixture over the meat and give it a good mix. Feel free to use your hands, to thoroughly get the marinade coated all over the meat.
4. Place bowl in the refrigerator for a minimum of 30 minutes, or overnight to allow all the flavours to emulsify.
5. After the meat has been left to marinate, thread the pieces of meat through the prepared bamboo or metal skewers.
6. Pre-heat grill to medium/high. Once heated, grill skewers, turning every 5 minutes to avoid charring, until nicely browned and thoroughly cooked. Keep an eye on them as each grill is different. If using the oven, cook at 375F for 40 minutes, turning the skewers halfway through.
7. Enjoy with your choice of salad or vegetables, Greek Keto Pita Bread, with tzatziki or simply on their own, without any sides, and as a quick protein snack.

MACROS: (per skewer about 220 g, 7 pieces of meat)
Calories: 340
Fat: 10.6 g / 29%
Protein: 57.1 g / 70.5%
Net Carbs: 0.48 g /0.5%

PASTITSADA - KOKKINISTO / VEAL POT ROAST and STEWED VEAL
My Greek Keto Kitchen: Traditional Dishes

Dairy Free

Nut Free

Prep Time: 20 minutes
Cook Time: 2 hours approximately
Servings: about 10 servings

*These popular dishes are served all over Greece! Pastitsada, or veal pot roast is a traditional dish from the Island of Corfu and is always served with pasta. This casserole dish is a Sunday dinner family favourite easily baked in the oven. We are using veal; however, you can use beef or pork, and many, have even used rooster (depending on the region in Greece one is from). Kokkinisto, which means "reddened" is another family favourite dish that consists of cubed veal (also works well with beef or pork) stewed in a red sauce on a stove top. Normally, you would see this dish served with rice, mashed potatoes, fried potatoes or pasta. Instead, you can enjoy it with cauliflower rice, cabbage noodles, zucchini noodles, Greek keto olive bread or Greek keto pita bread. (**See Page 130, 133 for the recipe**).*

Ingredients:

- About 4 lbs (2 kg) of veal shoulder, preferably with fat and bone in (or your choice of meat, but no lean meat)
- 1 large sized onion, finely chopped (about 1 cup - 150 g)
- 1 cup (250 ml) strained tomatoes, bottled or canned
- 1 can (796ml) diced tomatoes
- 5 garlic cloves, finely chopped
- 2 garlic cloves, sliced to stud meat *See NOTE BELOW
- 4 tbs butter
- 2 bay leaves
- 1/2 tsp cinnamon
- 1/4 tsp cloves
- 1 tbs apple cider vinegar
- 1 tsp pink Himalayan salt or sea salt (1/2 tsp for the sauce and 1/2 tsp to season meat)

- 16 pinches of black pepper (8 pinches for the sauce and 8 to season meat)
- 1 cup (about 100 g) of Kefalotiri or Parmesan cheese to sprinkle on each plate (optional)

Cooking Method:

1. Preheat your oven to 350F.
2. Finely chop the onion and 5 garlic cloves and set aside.
3. Slice the 2 garlic cloves. Make small cuts into the veal with a sharp knife and stud the garlic slices into the cuts. (Omit this step if making the veal stew).
4. Season your veal roast with 1/2 tsp of salt and 8 pinches of pepper.
5. Heat 2 tbs of the butter on medium high in a large skillet or bake proof pan and brown each side of the veal. Add more butter, if needed, but keep an eye on the meat to prevent from sticking to the pan. Remove from the pan when all sides are seared and set aside.
6. Add the onion with 2 tbs of butter on medium low heat and sauté until softened. Stir in cinnamon, cloves, chopped garlic and bay leaves to release the aromas and sauté for another minute. Add the tomato sauce, diced tomatoes, apple cider vinegar and the remainder of salt and pepper. Stir well and bring to a boil.
7. Lower heat and return the meat to the baking pan. Simmer for a couple of minutes on the stove top then transfer to the oven. Bake for about 1 to 1 1/2 hours or until the veal is tender and the sauce thickened. (You can also use a baking thermometer to ensure desired doneness). If making the stew, continue cooking on low heat on the stovetop for the same amount of time.
8. To serve, slice the desired portions, or serve the stew over your favourite side dish! Enjoy as well with grated Kefalotiri or Parmesan cheese!

*NOTE: Stud meat - make little incisions all over the meat and stuff pieces of garlic in the holes.

MACROS: (about 225 g per serving)
Calories: 528.7
Fat: 25 g / 42.3%
Protein: 65.5 g / 52.6%
Net Carbs: 6.73 g / 5%

Macros calculated without cheese

Whether you are using a pot roast or cubed meat, the ingredients indicated are the same. The cut of meat only varies. Macro-nutrients calculated using veal.

KOTOSOUPA ME AVGOLEMONO / CHICKEN SOUP with LEMON SAUCE

My Greek Keto Kitchen: Traditional Dishes

Dairy Free

Nut Free

Prep Time: 40 minutes
Cook Time: 2 hours approximately
Servings: 12

This traditional and lemony chicken soup is not only flavourful, but also loaded with many health benefits! Our grandmothers know best when they serve this up because it is full of vitamins and minerals, and very delicious. A bowl of old fashion chicken soup has been known for centuries to have natural healing properties for the body, mind and soul. But when you pair this with a creamy lemon sauce, you have just taken the nutrient level up a few more notches!

Ingredients:

- One whole chicken cut up into portions, mostly deboned. (Do not discard bones or skin *See NOTE BELOW)
- 1 tbs apple cider vinegar
- 2 bay leaves
- 1/2 tsp of pink Himalayan salt or sea salt
- 1/3 tsp of black pepper
- 1/4 tsp dried thyme
- 16 cups (4 litres) of water
- 2 leeks, sliced and including the green parts (about 2 cups – 180 g) **See NOTE BELOW
- 3 medium sized celery stalks sliced, (about 1 ½ cup - 120 g) (individual stocks not bunches)

Ingredients for lemon sauce:

- 3 large eggs (room temperature recommended as cold from the fridge can curdle the cream)
- Juice of two lemons (about 1/3 cup - 75ml)
- A couple of pinches of black pepper

Cooking Method:

1. Cut the chicken into pieces and debone as much as you can but save the BONES. (you can ask your butcher to do this for you).
2. Place meat in a dish and set aside for the time being while you make the chicken stock.
3. In a big pot, place all of the chicken bones, water, salt, pepper, bay leaves and thyme.
4. Bring to a boil over medium high heat. Once it's reached a boil, add the apple cider vinegar and simmer on low heat for about an hour. ***See NOTE BELOW
5. Skim froth with a slotted spoon, if necessary.
6. In the meantime, prepare vegetables, cut celery in slices and leeks as per note below.
7. Prepare chicken meat by cutting into pieces or strips.
8. Once the stock is ready, remove from heat.
9. Strain the stock by using a mesh colander and pour into a big bowl. Discard the bones.
10. Wash your pot and return to stove top.
11. Place chicken strips and vegetables into a pot and sauté the vegetables until soft, and the meat partially cooked. If meat starts to stick to the pan, add a little water.
12. Return the stock to the pot and bring to a boil. Once its reached boil point lower heat to medium low and simmer for about 30 minutes to allow the chicken to cook completely.
13. Once your soup is ready remove from heat and start preparing lemon sauce.
14. In a medium sized bowl whisk your eggs thoroughly.
15. Gradually add in the lemon juice while continuously whisking and the mixture thickens up and becomes creamy.
16. Add a half a ladle of the soup while continuing to whisk. ****See NOTE BELOW
17. Add about 5-6 more half ladle-fulls in the same manner. By adding one at a time and whisking thoroughly in between each addition.
18. At this point you should have a creamy egg lemon sauce. Pour all of the sauce from the bowl to the pot.
19. Season with pepper and salt to taste.

MACROS: (about 415 g per serving)
Calories: 150.5
Fat: 8.2 g / 49%
Protein: 15.5 g / 43.7%
Net Carbs: 2.45 g / 7.3%

*NOTE to save you time get your butcher to d-bone chicken for you or cut up yourself with a sharp knife. Does not have to be cut up equally.

**NOTE: Cut leeks into rounds and soak in cold water to remove dirt that sometimes accumulates. Drain and change water and repeat if needed until no dirt is left on leeks.

***NOTE: The apple cider vinegar assists to extract flavour and minerals from the bones.

****NOTE: This is an important step in making the creamy sauce. To ensure the sauce does not bake the eggs its best that the soup is not boiling but hot/warm.

MOUSSAKA / MEAT EGGPLANT CASSEROLE
My Greek Keto Kitchen: Traditional Dishes

Prep Time: 1h and 50 minutes approximately
Cook Time: 2h and 40 minutes approximately
Servings: 12

I am taking this classic casserole dish, that can be found all over Greece, and yes, I am going to show you how to **keto-fy** *it!! Hence, no potatoes or white flour for the bechamel sauce. This classic dish is definitely a favourite in our household because it is delicious, nutritious and low carb too. It might take a bit longer to make as it consists of a three-step process that includes the meat sauce, the eggplant layers, and the nutritious faux bechamel made with a cauliflower mash. Despite the time it requires to build, it is worth every minute. I recommend that you make it the day before or earlier in the day and re-heat the servings as you go. This tip is helpful if you would like to have cleanly cut squares when serving. Alternatively, when it is very hot, the individual servings will be very "loose" and fall apart. This is not necessary though; it will still taste delicious!*

Ingredients for Eggplants:

- 2 large eggplants (about 1.5 lbs – 700 g when cooked)
- 1tsp salt

Ingredients for Meat Sauce:

- About 3 lbs (1.4 kg) of medium ground beef
- 1 large onion, finely diced (about 1 cup – 150 g)
- 2 garlic cloves, finely minced
- 3 tbs unsalted butter
- 660ml bottle or can of strained tomatoes (pure tomatoes with no added sugars)
- 2 bay leaves
- 1/2 tsp of pink Himalayan salt or sea salt
- Ground black pepper, 6-8 pinches to taste
- 1 tsp dried oregano
- 1 tsp ground all spice
- 1 tsp ground cinnamon
- 2 tsp garlic powder
- 2 tbs apple cider vinegar

- 1 tbs Greek extra virgin olive oil
- 3 tbs fresh parsley, finely chopped

Ingredients for faux Bechamel (cauliflower mash):

- 1 large cauliflower chopped into florets (about 2.8 lbs – 1.3 kg when cooked)
- 1/2 tsp salt
- 1/4 tsp ground pepper
- 1 tbs garlic powder (plus 2 tsp for topping)
- 2 tbs unsalted butter
- 1/4 cup (57 g) cheddar cheese
- 1/4 cup (57 g) grated kefalotyri or Parmesan cheese (for topping)

Cooking Method for Eggplants:

1. Slice the eggplants into 1 cm rings and place in a colander. Sprinkle lightly with sea salt and give them a good mix with your hands. Set aside for about 30 minutes for the moisture to be drain out.
2. You may want to place on a towel or paper towel as well for about 15 minutes afterwards to remove a little more moisture.
3. Prepare two baking sheets with parchment paper. Lay the eggplant on the baking sheets and bake for about 20-30 minutes or until softened. You may also grill the eggplants or fry instead.
4. Once ready, set aside for assembly of casserole.

Cooking Method for Meat Sauce:

1. In a large pot, melt your butter over medium heat and add diced onion. Lower heat and stir frequently for about 5 minutes, keeping an eye on it so it does not burn.
2. Once the onion starts to soften, add the cinnamon, all spice, minced garlic and bay leaves and stir for about 5 minutes to release the aromas.
3. Now, add the ground beef while bringing the heat up to medium/high. Stir constantly to break up the meat and cook until it has browned.

4. Once thoroughly browned, add the tomato sauce, salt, pepper, oregano, garlic powder and bring to a boil. If needed, add in a little water. I usually add a little water by rinsing out the bottle of tomato sauce.
5. Once it has reached a boil, add the apple cider vinegar and simmer on low for about 45-60 minutes, or until the sauce has thickened. Towards the end (last 20 minutes), add in the Greek extra virgin olive oil.
6. Remove from heat, remove bay leaves and add in the fresh chopped parsley. Set aside until assembly time.

Cooking Method for faux Bechamel (Cauliflower Mash):

1. Place the cauliflower in a pot of water with a couple of pinches of salt. Boil until tender, then drain well in a colander.
2. Once drained, add the cauliflower back into the pot on medium heat, and mash with a potato masher.
3. Add the butter and seasonings
4. Add cheese
5. Season to taste with a little more salt, butter or cheese for a creamier taste and texture.

Cooking Method for the final assembly of the casserole dish:

1. Pre-heat your oven to 350F. Prepare an oven baking dish 11" x 15" (28cm x 38cm).
2. In the baking dish, spread a little meat sauce to cover most of the bottom.
3. Arrange one layer of the cooked eggplant across the baking dish. Carefully spoon in a layer of meat sauce on top of the eggplants. Repeat with the remainder of the eggplant and meat sauce following the same procedure.
4. Pour the cauliflower mash on top of the casserole dish and smooth it across with your spoon.
5. Sprinkle with your Kefalotyri or Parmesan cheese, and with the remainder of the garlic powder.

6. Bake for 45-60 minutes or until golden brown on top.
7. As mentioned above, I recommend that you cool the dish down completely before serving for easier cutting and serving. If you just can't wait, allow the dish to cool down for at least 15 minutes before serving.

MACROS: (per generous serving about 315 g)
Calories: 412.8
Fat: 26.4 g / 58.4%
Protein: 28.4 g / 27.1%
Net Carbs: 11.49 g / 14.5%

PASTITSIO / MEAT AND FAUX PASTA CASSEROLE
My Greek Keto Kitchen: Traditional Dishes

Prep Time: 45 minutes
Cook Time: 2h approximately
Servings: 12

This classic baked dish can be found all over Greece, and chances are, you have tried it once before yourself. It was one of my favourites growing up and it is still today! It might take a bit longer to make as it consists of a three-step process which is the meat sauce, pasta (faux), and a delicious bechamel sauce. However, it is worth every minute. I recommend that you make it the day before you intend to serve it, or earlier in the day if for dinner, and heat it up as you go. This tip will ensure neat and clean-cut squares when serving, because when this dish is served hot from the oven, the individual servings will be very "loose" and fall apart. Making ahead is optional however and won't affect the flavours. It will still taste delicious!

Ingredients for Meat Sauce:

- About 3 lbs (1.4 kg) of medium ground beef
- 1 large onion, finely diced (about 1 cup – 150 g)
- 2 garlic cloves, finely minced
- 3 tbs of unsalted butter
- 1 bottle or can strained tomatoes 660ml (pure tomatoes with no added sugars)
- 2 bay leaves
- 1/2 tsp of pink Himalayan salt or sea salt
- ground black pepper, to taste
- 1 tsp dried oregano
- 1 tsp ground allspice
- 1 tsp ground cinnamon
- 2 tsp garlic powder
- 2 tbs apple cider vinegar
- 1 tbs Greek extra virgin olive oil
- 3 tbs fresh parsley, finely chopped

Ingredients for faux Pasta Noodles:

- 1 small to medium cabbage, sliced in long strips like noodles (about 2 lbs - 880 g when cooked)
- 1/2 tsp of pink Himalayan salt or sea salt
- ground black pepper, to taste
- 5 tbs of unsalted butter
- 3 large eggs lightly beaten
- 3 tbs grated Kefalotiri or Parmesan cheese
- 3 tbs of fresh parsley, finely chopped

Ingredients for Bechamel Sauce:

- 2 cups (480 ml) unsweetened almond milk (or your choice of unsweetened nut milk)
- 2 cups (480 ml) heavy cream (35% cream)
- 8 tbs unsalted butter
- 1 cup (112 g) almond flour
- 2 cups (226 g) grated Cheddar cheese
- 2.5 ounces (70 g)cream cheese (full fat)
- 1/4 cup (57 g) grated Kefalotiri or Parmesan cheese (for topping)
- 4 tsp garlic powder (reserve 2 tsp for topping)
- 1/2 tsp pink Himalayan salt or sea salt
- 2 bay leaves
- 1/2 tsp of ground allspice
- 1/2 tsp ground nutmeg
- 8 dashes of ground black pepper (or to taste)

Cooking Method for Meat Sauce:

1. In a large pot, melt butter over medium heat and add diced onion. Lower heat and stir frequently. Keep an eye on it so that it does not burn. Cook for about 5 minutes or until onion is soft and translucent.
2. Add to onion, cinnamon, allspice, minced garlic and bay leaves and stir together for about 1 minute to release the aromas.
3. Add the ground beef while bringing the heat up to medium/high. Stir constantly to break up the meat and cook until browned.
4. Once thoroughly browned, add tomato sauce, salt, pepper, oregano, garlic powder and bring to a boil. If needed, add in a little water. A good tip is to add a little water to the empty bottle of tomato sauce, gently shake, and add it to the pot.
5. Once it reaches a boil, add the apple cider vinegar and simmer on low for about 45-60 minutes or until the sauce has thickened. Towards the end - the last 20 minutes, add in the Greek extra virgin olive oil.
6. Remove from heat, remove bay leaves and add in the fresh chopped parsley. Set aside until assembly time.

Cooking Method for faux Pasta Noodles:

1. Pre-heat oven to 350F.
2. Add the cabbage "noodles" and place in an oven baking dish 11" x 15" (28cm x 38cm).
3. Add salt, pepper and 3 tbs of the unsalted butter and place in a hot oven. After 15-20 minutes, give the cabbage a good mix and add in the remainder of the butter. Keep an eye on the dish and mix occasionally. Bake until slightly tender, about 30-40 minutes. The doneness will depend on the thickness of the faux noodles, but we are going for al dente "noodles".
4. Remove from the oven and add the fresh chopped parsley.
5. Allow to cool.
6. Once cooled, add in the lightly beaten eggs and the cheese. Mix the faux pasta well. *Note ensure the noodles have cooled down to avoid cooking the egg and only do this last step when you are ready to assemble the casserole.

Cooking Method for Bechamel Sauce:

1. In a medium pot and over low heat, add the unsweetened almond milk, 35% cream, bay leaves and allspice.
2. In another larger pot, melt the butter and add almond flour and whisk for about 5 minutes or until well combined. * Be careful to not burn.
3. Discard the bay leaves, and slowly ladle the warm dairy mixture into the flour mixture while whisking constantly and until there are no lumps.
4. Add the cream cheese and whisk until the sauce has thickened.
5. Remove from heat, add cheddar cheese, garlic powder, salt, pepper and nutmeg. Give it a good mix.

Cooking Method for the final assembly of the casserole dish:

1. Pre-heat oven to 350F.
2. In the already cooked faux noodle baking dish that has cooled down, add the prepared meat sauce by spreading it across the noodles until completely covered.
3. Carefully spoon in the bechamel sauce on top of the meat sauce and smooth over the casserole dish until completely covered.
4. Sprinkle with Kefalotiri or Paremesan cheese and the remaining 2 tsps. of garlic powder.
5. Bake for 45-60 minutes or until the top is golden brown.
6. As mentioned above, I recommend to completely cool the dish for easier slicing and serving. Otherwise, allow to cool down for at least 15 minutes before serving.

MACROS: (per generous serving, about 320 g)
Calories: 709.8
Fat: 56.7 g / 71.9%
Protein: 35.1 g / 20%
Net Carbs: 11.75 g / 8.1%

SOUTZOUKAKIA / GREEK MEATBALLS IN A TOMATO SAUCE

My Greek Keto Kitchen: Traditional Dishes

Dairy Free

Nut Free

Prep Time: 60 minutes (for both)
Cook Time: 40 minutes (for meatballs) 60 minutes for (sauce)
Servings: about 30 meatballs

These football-shaped meatballs are full of aromatic flavours! Adding them to a savoury sauce adds that extra deliciousness!! These pleasant scents remind me of our family Greek kitchen growing up.   This time around, we opted for veal instead of beef, which I recommend you give a try. Feel free however, to use your choice of ground meat or combination, just make sure it is not the lean variety.   The original recipe calls for bread soaking in milk; however, we are omitting it completely to "Ketofy" the recipe. To tell you the truth, if you ever tried the original recipe you couldn't tell the difference. Normally, this dish is served with rice, instead, try it with cauliflower rice, Greek Keto Olive Bread or Greek Keto Pita Bread. (See page 130, 133 for the recipe).

Ingredients for Meatballs:

- About 4.4 lbs (2 kg) of ground veal (or your choice of ground meat, do not use lean meat)
- 1 large onion, finely chopped (about 1 cup – 150 g)
- 3 tsp ground cumin
- 2 tbs fresh mint, finely chopped
- 6 garlic cloves, finely chopped
- 4 tbs Greek extra virgin olive oil
- 2 tsp pink Himalayan salt or sea salt
- 4 - 6 pinches of black pepper
- 3 eggs, beaten

Ingredients for Tomato Sauce:

- 1 can diced tomatoes (790ml)
- 1 bottle or can strained tomatoes (680ml)
- 1 1/4 cups (300 ml) water
- 3 tbs unsalted butter
- 2 tbs Greek extra virgin olive oil
- 1 tsp apple cider vinegar
- 1 large onion, finely chopped (about 1 cup – 150 g)
- 1/4 tsp ground cinnamon
- 2 bay leaves
- 3 garlic cloves, finely chopped
- 5 fresh basil leaves, finely chopped
- 1/2 tsp pink Himalayan salt or sea salt
- 3 - 4 pinches of black pepper
- 1 tsp dried oregano

Cooking Method:

1. Place veal in a bowl.
2. Finely chop the onion, mint, garlic and add to the bowl. Add the rest of the ingredients and mix well. Feel free to mix or knead with your hands or use a big spoon.
3. Place bowl with meat mixture in the refrigerator for about 30 minutes to allow all the flavours to emulsify.
4. Prepare 2 lined baking sheets (size does not matter for the baking sheets)
5. Form into football shaped meatballs by rolling into long oval shapes with your hand. They are approximately 70 grams each.
6. Pre-heat oven to 375F and bake for 40 minutes or until cooked through and slightly browned on top. Keep an eye on them as each oven heats different and you may need less or more time. Halfway through the baking, switch the baking sheets from top to bottom and vice versa for even cooking. While the meatballs are baking start preparing the tomato sauce.

Cooking Method for Tomatoe Sauce:

1. Finely chop the onion, garlic and fresh basil.
2. Heat the butter in a big pot or skillet on medium heat. It should be big enough to make sauce and to hold the 30 meatballs.
3. Add the onion and sauté until caramelized. Stir frequently, and if needed, lower the heat so it does not burn.
4. Add the garlic and sauté until softened, along with the cinnamon, bay leaves and stir to release the aromas.
5. Add the diced and strained tomatoes, salt, pepper, oregano and water. Bring it to a boil. Once it reaches a boil reduce the heat to low and simmer for about 40 to 50 minutes. We are looking for a rich thick sauce.
6. About 30 minutes into simmering, add the olive oil and apple cider vinegar.
7. Remove bay leaves. Once sauce has thickened and meatballs are fully baked, add one meatball at a time (see note below) into the pot. Simmer all together for about 10 minutes to allow all the wonderful flavours to blend.
8. If needed, season with more salt and/or pepper. Add chopped fresh basil.

MACROS: (about 70 g per meatball)
Calories: 164
Fat: 8 g / 43.6%
Protein: 18.4 g / 47.7%
Net Carbs: 3.55 g / 8.8%

*NOTE: At times when baking meat in the oven, due to excess liquid/fat, a layer of fat may accumulate around the meatballs. Just remove it before placing them in the tomato sauce.

*Macros calculated using ground veal.

SPANAKORIZO / SPINACH RICE
My Greek Keto Kitchen: Traditional Dishes

Dairy Free

Nut Free

Prep Time: 20 minutes
Cook Time: 30 minutes
Servings: 4

This traditional one pot meal brings a flood of memories as a young girl in my mom's kitchen. I remember eating it during times of Lent, and truth be told, I was not a huge fan at the time. With time, it became a taste I longed for and it has now become one of my favourites as a revised Keto and Low carb version. So, what are we replacing the rice with? You guessed it, cauliflower rice!! I recommend adding some crumbled Feta cheese or a hard cheese like Parmesan to add a little more texture to the already flavourful dish. *Please note that the macros do not include the crumbled cheese.

Ingredients:

- About 2.2 lbs (1 kg) of frozen spinach
- About 1 lbs (454 g) of cauliflower (one small cauliflower head or half of a large one)
- 4 tbs (about 50 g) of butter or avocado oil
- 3 tbs fresh dill, finely chopped
- 1 small onion, minced (about 1/2 cup - 60 g)
- 1 bunch fresh green onions, chopped with green stems
- 2 to 3 garlic cloves, finely chopped
- 2 tbs fresh lemon juice
- ½ tsp pink Himalayan salt or sea salt, or season to taste
- 2 to 3 pinches of black pepper, or season to taste

Cooking Method:

1. Place Frozen Spinach in a colander to thaw out slightly too release some of its water (we want some of the liquid)
2. Wash Cauliflower and cut into florets. Place florets into a food processor (in batches not all at once) and Slowly PULSE until Cauliflower resembles rice. *NOTE: Be cautious to not over pulse cauliflower if not it will become a mash (It happened to me a couple of times and learned my lesson to not rush this step and to use the PULSE function and not chop/blend). Set aside.
3. Heat a medium sized skillet/sauce pan with a couple tablespoons of butter on medium high. Saute small onion until translucent (about 5 minutes) and than add green onions and saute a little more (about 2 minutes).
4. Add the semi frozen spinach and cook on medium low heat
5. Add in salt and black pepper
6. Once the mixture starts to cook through and loose most of its liquid add the Cauliflower Rice. As well add in the garlic, fresh dill, lemon juice and the remainder of butter. Stir frequently as we do not want it too stick to our skillet/sauce pan. *If needed add a little more butter to not stick. We do not want to over cook the Cauliflower Rice as if not it will turn into a mash.
7. Taste and adjust salt, pepper and lemon juice to your liking
8. Once ready to serve add Feta Cheese, Parmesan or nutritional yeast (*optional)

MACROS: (per serving, about 400 g)
Calories: 212.1
Fat: 12.7 g / 51.9%
Protein: 12.5 g / 14.5%
Net Carbs: 8.13 g / 33.6%

*macros are based on using butter and without any of the cheeses or nutritional yeast.

SPANAKOPITAKIA / SPINACH PIES
My Greek Keto Kitchen: Traditional Dishes

Prep Time: 2h (depending on your level of ease of rolling out dough)
Cook Time: 40 minutes
Servings: about 22 pies

These famous spinach pies are known world-wide, and you have certainly come across them at your favourite restaurant or Greek home. It consists of a delightfully phyllo dough filled with delicious feta cheese, spinach and seasonings! Many eat this for breakfast, as a snack or as a meal with salad or other side dishes. There are as many versions of this recipe circulating as there are regions of Greece. With a little experimenting we took my mom's family recipe and ketofied it!! They do take a little time to make, just like the non-Keto version, however, your family and friends will be asking for more!

Ingredients for the dough:

- 2 cups (224 g) almond flour
- 2/3 cup (100 g) coconut flour
- 1/3 cup (55 g) psyllium husk powder
- 1/2 tsp of salt
- 1 tbs apple cider vinegar
- 1/2 cup (118 ml) Greek extra virgin olive oil
- 1 to 2 cups warm water (250 ml -500 ml) (you are looking for a sticky but firm consistency to form a ball so keep that in mind when adding water: I used 1 ¾ cups – 425 ml)

Ingredients for the filling:

- 9.5 oz (270 g) Greek feta cheese, crumbled
- 3 bunches of fresh spinach washed and trimmed (about 6 cups - 900 g before cooking, 3 cups - 400 g once cooked and drained). * Spinach found in packaged bags helps with the quantity.
- 4 large eggs, beaten
- 6 green onions, finely chopped including green stems

- 4 tbs fresh dill, finely chopped
- Salt and black pepper to taste

Ingredients for egg wash:

- 1 large egg, beaten

Preparation Method for the dough:

1. In a bowl, mix with a spoon all of your dry ingredients: almond flour, coconut flour, salt and psyllium husk powder.
2. Add the apple cider vinegar to the flour mixture and stir with a spoon. Gradually add the olive oil and continue mixing.
3. You may now want to use a spatula or your hands to mix the dough while slowly adding the warm water. Remember, not to over-water. We are looking for a wet dough that easily forms into a ball.
4. Place a towel over the dough and put aside for about 20 minutes.

Preparation Method for the Filling and baking the spanakopites:

1. While the dough is resting prepare the filling.
2. In a skillet, cook spinach until wilted, add in the green onions and cook all together until spinach is thoroughly cooked and water has been completely absorbed. *Note the spinach leaves water so there is no need to add any oil or liquid to the skillet. You may wish to add a little water or oil if spinach and onions have not fully cooked and the mixture is sticking to the skillet.
3. Once ready, transfer to a colander to drain thoroughly and to cool completely. *You can use the back of a spoon or your hands to squeeze out any excess liquid.
4. In a medium bowl using a fork or hands, crumble the feta. Add in finely chopped dill, black pepper and the beaten eggs. Mix well.
5. Once the spinach mixture has completely cooled, add to the cheese and egg mixture. Mix well and if needed, add a little salt.

6. Prepare 2 lined baking sheets with either silicone mats or parchment paper.
7. Prepare 2 sheets of parchment paper to roll out dough into small pies with a rolling pin.
8. While keeping hands wet with warm water (have a bowl close by), roll out dough into tennis-size balls and then gently flatten on parchment paper with your hands. Place the other parchment paper on top and roll out between the two parchment papers to an approximate 2mm thickness.
9. Nothing fancy is required to cut out circle shapes. I used a coffee mug with a diameter of 10cm or 4inches. Lightly press your mug or other round tool into the dough by first removing the top parchment paper. After cutting out your circle. If needed, roll out the dough to the thinness we are looking for by first replacing the top parchment paper.
10. Spoon some of the filling, about 2 tbs, or just enough to be able to fold over the dough to make a half moon shape. Slightly press with wet fingers to seal the spinach pie over the fold of the half moon. Place on the lined baking sheet.
11. Brush the egg wash on each spanakopitaki or spinach pie. Repeat steps until all the dough has been used.
12. Bake at 375F for about 30 minutes or golden brown. Alternate the baking sheets half-way through to ensure even baking. Enjoy warm or cold, depending on your preference. I love them warm, myself!

MACROS: (per pie)
Calories: 192.9
Fat: 14.8 g / 70.5%
Protein: 6.9 g / 14.5%
Net Carbs: 1.76 g / 15%

TIROPITAKIA / CHEESE PIES
My Greek Keto Kitchen: Traditional Dishes

Prep Time: 2h (depending on your level of ease of rolling out dough)
Cook Time: 40 minutes
Servings: about 22 pies

These famous cheese pies are known world-wide, and you have certainly come across them at your favourite restaurant or Greek home. These delicious beauties are very similar to the Spanakopitakia recipe but with a few additional ingredients. They consist of a similarly delightful phyllo dough filled with delicious feta cheese and ricotta, and seasonings including mint! They are so versatile that many enjoy these for breakfast, as well as an afternoon snack or as a meal with salad or other side dishes. As there are many region-specific recipes for similar dishes, you will find a few variations of this recipe. We've always enjoyed my mom's family recipe but now, I've ketofied it to be low carb, but equally delicious!

Ingredients for the dough:

- 2 cups (224 g) almond flour
- 2/3 cup (100 g) coconut flour
- 1/3 cup (55 g) psyllium husk powder
- 2 to 3 pieces Mastiha* spice, ground (optional)
- 1/2 tsp of sea salt
- 1 tbs apple cider vinegar
- 1/2 cup (113.5 g) melted butter
- 1 to 2 cups boiled warm water (250 ml -500 ml) (You are looking for a sticky but firm consistency to form a ball so keep that in mind when adding water: I used 1 ¾ cups – 425 ml)

Ingredients for the filling:

- 7 oz (200g) Greek feta, crumbled
- 7 oz (200g) Ricotta cheese
- 2 large eggs, beaten
- pinch of black pepper
- 2 tbs fresh mint, finely chopped

Ingredients for egg wash:

- 1 large egg beaten

Preparation Method for the dough:

1. In a bowl, mix with a spoon all of the dry ingredients, almond flour, coconut flour, salt and psyllium husk powder.
2. If adding, using a mortar to avoid sticking, grind the mastiha with a couple of pinches of salt, then add it to the melted butter.
3. Add the apple cider vinegar to the flour and stir with a spoon. Gradually add the melted butter with the mastiha to the flour mixture and continue mixing.
4. You may now want to use a spatula or your hands to mix the dough while slowly adding the warm water. Remember, not to over-water. We are looking for a wet dough that easily forms into a ball.
5. Place a towel over the dough and set aside for about 20 minutes.

Preparation Method for the Filling and baking the tiropites:

1. While the dough is resting, prepare the filling.
2. In a medium bowl, using a fork, crumble the feta. Add in the ricotta cheese, finely chopped mint, black pepper and the beaten eggs. Mix well.
3. Prepare 2 lined baking sheets with either silicone mats or parchment paper.
4. Prepare 2 sheets of parchment paper to roll out dough into small pies with a rolling pin.
5. While keeping hands wet with warm water (have a bowl close by), roll out dough into tennis-size balls and then gently flatten on parchment paper with your hands. Place the other parchment paper on top and roll out between the two parchment papers to an approximate 2mm thickness.
6. Nothing fancy is required to cut out circle shapes. I used a coffee mug with a diameter of 10cm or 4inches. Lightly press your mug or other round tool into the dough by first removing the top parchment paper. After cutting out your circle. If needed, roll out the dough to the thinness we are looking for by first replacing the top parchment paper.

7. Spoon some of the filling, about 1 1/2 tbs, or just enough to be able to fold over the dough to make a half moon shape. Slightly press with wet fingers to seal the cheese pie over the fold of the half moon. Place on the lined baking sheet.

8. Brush the egg wash on each tiropitaki / cheese pie. Repeat steps until all the dough has been used. *If any dough is left over and you run out of filling, form into mini buns or flat bread.

9. Bake at 375F for about 30 minutes or golden brown. Alternate the baking sheets half-way through to ensure even baking. Enjoy warm or cold, depending on your preference. I love them warm, myself!

Notes*

HEALTH BENEFITS OF MASTIHA:

Mastic gum is the resin of the evergreen mastic tree, native to the Chios island in Greece where it is known as 'mastiha'. Scientific research has shown that this resin has antioxidant, anti-bacterial, and anti-inflammatory qualities. This powerful, magical and natural resin has been known to have many health benefits including improving digestion, lowering LDL cholesterol levels, improve dental health, reduce acid reflux and much, much more. It is also known to be the very first natural chewing gum in human, as well as an aromatic spice enjoyed in many recipes. Today, it is still chewed as well as used in *pharmaceuticals, cosmetics,* and in the *culinary* world.

MACROS: (per pie)
Calories: 177.6
Fat: 13.7 g / 70.2%
Protein: 5.9 g / 13.8%
Net Carbs: 2.08 g / 16%

DESSERTS & BREADS

AMYGDALOTA / GREEK ALMOND COOKIES

My Greek Keto Kitchen – Desserts and Breads

Dairy Free

Prep Time: 40 minutes
Cook Time: 25 minutes
Servings: 30 Cookies

Whether you are Greek or not, I am sure you have either tried or purchased amygdalota (almond cookies) from a Greek bakery. I remember as a child, these were my first choice when walking into a Greek bakery. These cookies are crunchy on the outside and oh, so chewy on the inside. They are the perfect sweet treat for any occasion!

Ingredients:

- 4 large egg whites
- 1 cup (about 200 g) monk fruit & erythritol blend (feel free to use your choice of low carb sugar substitute)
- 4 cups (448 g) almond flour
- 1/8 tsp sea salt
- 1 tsp pure almond extract
- 1 tsp vanilla extract
- 30 whole or sliced almonds

Baking Method:

1. Preheat oven to 325F.
2. Line 2 cookie sheets with parchment paper or silicone baking mats.
3. In a medium sized bowl, beat the egg whites with 1/2 tbs of low carb sugar substitute and half the salt (1/16 tsp) on medium speed until they form soft peaks. Then add the extracts and set aside.
4. In a large bowl, combine the almond flour, the remaining low carb sugar substitute and salt.

5. Fold the egg white mixture into the almond flour mixture until a dough is formed.
6. Roll dough between the palm of your hands into walnut size balls and place them on the prepared cookie sheets.
7. Flatten each ball slightly by pushing your thumb into the dough to form a dimple. Place a whole almond or some sliced almonds in the middle of the dimple.
8. Bake for about 20 to 25 minutes or until slightly golden brown. Halfway through the time, rotate the cookie sheets from top to bottom for even baking.
9. Allow to cool down completely on a baking rack and note that these cookies will harden as they cool down. Store them at room temperature in an airtight container if they will be consumed within 7 days, otherwise store them in the fridge to retain freshness.

MACROS: (per cookie)
Calories: 95
Fat: 8.1 g / 74.2%
Protein: 4.2 g / 17.4%
Net Carbs: 1.67 g / 7.5%

GALAKTOBOUREKO / CUSTARD PIES

My Greek Keto Kitchen: Desserts and Breads

Dairy Free

Prep Time: 30 minutes
Cook Time: 25 minutes
Servings: 4

This Greek classic dessert is known by many across the globe. My grandfather, God bless his soul, used to have a pet name for me - "galaktoboureko". I am not sure why, but perhaps because my skin was white as "gala" - which means milk. So, for this and many other reasons, it was important for me to come up with a keto approved alternative in his loving memory. So, then Pappou Gabrillo (Grandfather), this one is for you!! There is no need for a syrup or a phyllo dough, as the flavours in the custard are satisfying enough. Not only did I go against the grain on this one, but it is dairy free as well.

Ingredients:

- 2 cans (400 ml each) full fat coconut milk (yields approximately 2 cups after some water is drained)
- 4 large egg yolks
- 1/4 cup (about 50 g) monk fruit & erythritol blend (feel free to use your choice of low carb sugar substitute)
- Pinch Himalayan salt
- 1/2 tsp vanilla extract
- 1/2 cup (56 g) almond flour
- Zest from one lemon

Baking Method:

1. Preheat oven to 325F.
2. Drain one can of the coconut milk of its excess liquid but keep the liquid from the second. Pour them both in a saucepan and bring to a slow boil. Once the coconut cream comes to a simmer, remove it from the heat.

3. To the coconut milk, add a pinch of salt, vanilla extract, lemon zest and almond flour. Mix well with a spoon. Allow to cool.
4. In a large bowl, beat the egg yolks with sugar substitute until well combined and has a creamy texture.
5. Slowly pour the coconut mixture into the bowl with the egg mixture, while whisking. Once mixed well, place the combined mixture back into the saucepan and cook on low heat for about 10 minutes, stirring occasionally. Be careful that it does not overflow. Once thickened, remove from the heat and divide the mixture between four ramekins.
6. Place a paper towel at the bottom of a deep oven proof baking dish to keep the ramekins from moving. Place them in the dish and pour the boiling water around them until it reaches 3/4 of the way up the sides of the ramekins.
7. Bake for about 20 minutes or until set, but still wobbly.
8. At this point, if you want a little extra sweetness, sprinkle with your choice of sugar substitute and put on broil for about 5 minutes. If you do, keep an eye out not to burn them.
9. Remove the baking dish from oven and let it cool. Once cooled you can enjoy the custard cups at room temperature or place them in the fridge for a cold treat later.

MACROS: (per serving)
Calories: 413.2
Fat: 39.9 g / 87%
Protein: 7.6 g / 7.6%
Net Carbs: 2.89 g / 5%

Ensure the coconut mixture has cooled before adding to the egg mixture. You want it warm not hot. Extreme heat will leave you with scrambled eggs.

KOULOURAKIA / GREEK BUTTER COOKIES
My Greek Keto Kitchen: Desserts and Breads

Prep Time: 60 minutes
Cook Time: 25 minutes
Servings: 24 cookies

Who has heard of "koulourakia"? If you are not Greek, perhaps you know of someone who is and may have tried one before. These Greek cookies are typically baked during the Easter Holiday, but many enjoy making them year-round. As usual, I wanted to honor the family tradition without the guilt and so, my mom's family recipe passed on to her from her mother, has now been KeTofied!

Ingredients:

- 4 large eggs, separated
- 1 cup (about 200 g) monk fruit & erythritol blend (feel free to use your choice of low carb sugar substitute)
- 1 cup (227 g) unsalted butter, melted
- 1/2 cup (118 ml) warm unsweetened vanilla almond milk
- 2 cups and 1/4 cup (252 g) almond flour
- 1 cup (140 g) coconut flour
- 1/3 cup (55 g) psyllium husk powder (grind in a coffee grinder, otherwise use powder variety)
- 2 1/2 tbs baking powder
- 1 1/2 tsp of vanilla extract

Ingredients for egg wash:

- 2 large egg yolks
- 2 drops vanilla stevia (or regular stevia)

Baking Method:

1. Preheat oven to 350F and line cookie sheets with parchment paper or silicone baking mats.

2. Beat the egg yolks with the erythritol & monk fruit blend. Add the melted butter and beat until well combined and with a creamy consistency.
3. Add the warm milk, vanilla and baking powder, and give it a quick mix. Set aside and allow it to absorb, as warm milk will react with the baking powder.
4. In a large bowl, mix the remainder of the dry ingredients with a spoon (the almond flour, coconut flour and psyllium).
5. In a separate bowl, beat the egg whites until they form stiff peaks like a meringue, and set aside. *I find cold egg whites form stiff peaks easier.
6. Slowly add the dry ingredients (mixed flours) to the wet ingredients (egg yolk mixture) and mix well until completely combined and a cookie batter is formed.
7. With a spatula, fold egg whites slowly into the cookie batter.
8. To form the cookies in the traditional twist or braided method, I recommend you use a piece of parchment paper or a cutting board to roll it out. Take a spoon full of cookie dough and roll it into a walnut size ball in the palm of your hands. Now on either the parchment paper or the cutting board, place the cookie dough ball down and roll it into a worm-like shape. Repeat and form another. Each should measure about 3 inches in length. Place one end to the other and slowly cross one over the other similar to braiding but with 2 strands instead of 3. This takes practice as the dough is fragile since there is no gluten holding it together. If it breaks, try to patch it up by pinching and moulding it while in the twist.
9. Place them on a lined cookie sheet with space in between them as they will rise.
10. With a fork, beat the 2 egg yolks with stevia drops. Slightly brush the egg wash on each cookie.
11. Bake for about 20-25 minutes or until slightly browned.
12. Allow to cool down completely to get that signature Koulouraki texture of slightly crunchy on the outside, and soft and tender on the inside. Store these cookies at room temperature in a cookie jar-like container if consumed within 5 days otherwise use an airtight container and store in the fridge.

MACROS: (per cookie)
Calories: 181.1
Fat: 15.1 g / 74.1%
Protein: 4.3 g / 9.6%
Net Carbs: 2.04 g / 15.9%

Feel free to make any shape. You can make logs and with a knife make criss-cross pattern. Or even make a traditional cookie and flatten with your hand.

KOURABIEDES / GREEK SHORTBREAD COOKIES
My Greek Keto Kitchen: Desserts and Breads

Prep Time: 70 minutes (including freezer time)
Cook Time: 20 minutes
Servings: 30 Cookies

These traditional cookies have many names, such as "Wedding Cookies", "Sugar Cookies" and even "Christmas Cookies". To me, they spell childhood memories at their best! These buttery and crumbly cookies make them the perfect treat for any occasion or to fill up your cookie-jar for the any-time-of day yummy-ness! I am excited to share my family's recipe with you, but with a twist!

Ingredients:

- 3 cups (336 g) almond flour
- 1 cup (about 140 g) low carb confectioners' sweetener (*See Baking Tip page 23)
- 1 cup (227 g) unsalted butter (room temperature)
- 2 cups (240 g) walnuts, chopped (**See NOTE below)
- 1/2 tsp sea salt
- 4 drops vanilla stevia
- 2 tsp of vanilla extract
- Extra confectioners' sweetener to powder the cookies
- 1-2 tbs of rose water (this is optional, my family's recipe calls for it)

Baking Method:

1. Line 2 baking sheets with parchment paper or silicone baking mats (leave ample space in between so, I recommend 12 on each baking sheet, and if needed, a third with 6*).
2. Place all ingredients into a food processor, except for the walnuts and blend until the mixture has formed a dough.
3. Add in the chopped walnuts and pulse to not over process the nuts.
4. Taste the dough and adjust the sweetness to your taste. Remember that you will be adding confectioners' sweetener on top of cookies.
5. Scoop the dough and form into golf size balls by rolling in between the palm of your hands.

6. Place on prepared baking sheets (*if you need a third sheet but don't have one, place the extra 6 aside and bake after the 2 first baking sheets are ready).
7. Place the cookie sheets in the freezer for about 30-40 minutes.
8. Preheat oven to 350F.
9. Bake for about 15-20 minutes or until golden brown around the edges. Halfway through the baking, rotate the baking sheets from the top to bottom rack for even baking, but keep an eye on them. Repeat, if needed with a third baking sheet.
10. Allow the cookies to cool down on the baking sheets. These cookies will harden as they cool down.
11. When slightly cooled, brush the cookies lightly with the rose water.
12. When completely cooled, sift your choice of approved low carb confectioners' sugar.
13. Store these cookies at room temperature in an airtight container if consumed within 7 days otherwise, store them in the fridge.

MACROS: (per cookie)
Calories: 174.6
Fat: 17.1 g / 86%
Protein: 4.1 g / 9.1%
Net Carbs: 1.14 g / 4.5%

You can use pecans, pistachios or even almonds instead of walnuts. However, please note that this will change the macro nutrients.

RAVANI / ALMOND COCONUT CAKE
My Greek Keto Kitchen: Desserts and Breads

Prep Time: 20 minutes
Cook Time: 40 minutes
Servings: 15

This syrupy, fluffy, moist and citrus Greek traditional sponge cake can be found throughout Greece in different variations. Since semolina resembles almond flour in texture and in how it reacts in dough-making, with a few tweaks, I was able to turn this dessert into a delightful Keto-approved treat!

Ingredients for the syrup:

- 1/2 cup (about 100 g) monk fruit & erythritol blend (feel free to use your choice of low carb sugar substitute)
- 4 drops liquid vanilla stevia
- 2 1/2 cups (600 ml) water
- Rinds from one large lemon

Ingredients for the cake:

- 2 1/2 cups (280 g) almond flour
- 1/2 cup (70 g) coconut flour
- About 2 cups (150 g) unsweetened shredded coconut
- 1 cup (227 g) unsalted butter (softened at room temperature)
- 1 cup (about 200 g) monk fruit & erythritol blend (feel free to use your choice of low carb sweetener)
- 5 large eggs
- 2 tsp baking powder
- 1 tsp vanilla extract
- ½ tsp orange extract
- Pinch of sea salt or Himalayan salt

Cooking Method for the Syrup:

1. In a pot, add the water, sugar and lemon rinds.
2. Place over medium high heat and bring to a boil, stirring occasionally.
3. Once the simple syrup comes to a boil, remove from the heat and add the 4 drops of liquid vanilla stevia.
4. Stir and set aside to completely cool down.

Baking Method for the Cake:

1. Preheat oven to 350F and line a 9.8" x 13.7" (25cm x 35cm) baking pan with parchment paper.
2. In a large bowl, beat softened butter with sugar substitute until fluffy.
3. Add one egg at a time, orange extract, vanilla extract and beat until well combined.
4. In a separate bowl, combine dry ingredients: almond flour, coconut flour, shredded coconut, baking powder and salt.
5. Add dry ingredients slowly to the wet ingredients and blend until well combined.
6. Pour cake batter into the lined baking pan and spread evenly. If needed, wet your hands with a little water and spread evenly (the dough is thick and sticky, and the water helps the batter not stick to your hands).
7. Bake for about 40 minutes or until golden brown.
8. Once ready, remove immediately from the oven and with a ladle, pour the cooled syrup over the hot ravani.
9. Set it aside to allow the sponge cake to soak up the syrup and to cool. Enjoy!

MACROS: (per piece)
Calories: 339.3
Fat: 30.5 g / 80.3%
Protein: 7.5 g / 9.1%
Net Carbs: 2.87 g / 10.3%

For optimal results don't use a larger baking pan otherwise your ravani will be too thin.

VASILOPITA / GREEK NEW YEAR'S CAKE
My Greek Keto Kitchen: Desserts and Breads

Prep Time: 30 minutes
Cook Time: 60 minutes
Servings: 15

Depending which Greek family tradition you follow, you will enjoy a Vasilopita (King's Cake) on New Year's Day in either a bread or cake form. My mom baked a dense and citrus cake, and of course as tradition dictates, hid a coin in the dough before baking. This cake is associated with Saint Basil, who was a fierce defender of the Christian church. He died on January 1ˢᵗ 379AD, and in his honor we exchange gifts on that day instead of on December 25ᵗʰ. Our Vasilopita is made as well on this day to celebrate his life. It is a wonderful custom where each member of the family receives a piece after the head of the family cuts a slice while calling out their name. Personally, we choose our own piece after my husband slices the cake. It is said that whomever finds the coin in their piece, will have a very auspicious and abundant year ahead! Truth be told, this cake is so delicious and guilt-free that you can enjoy it anytime of the year – with or without the coin!

Ingredients:

- 2 1/4 cups (252 g) almond flour
- 1/2 cup (70 g) coconut flour
- 1 cup (227 g) unsalted butter (softened at room temperature)
- 8 oz (226.8 g) cream cheese (softened at room temperature)
- 1 1/4 cup (about 250 g) monk fruit & erythritol blend (feel free to use your choice of low carb sugar substitute)
- 10 large eggs
- 2 tsp baking powder
- 2 tsp vanilla extract
- 2 tsp almond extract
- 3 tsp orange liquor (you could omit; however, I feel that this gives it the distinct citrus flavour)
- 1/3 cup of sliced almonds (to decorate top of cake with the year number or "Happy New Year") This amount may vary, depending how large your number design will be.
- 2 tbs powdered low carb sugar (to decorate top of cake)

Baking Method:

1. Preheat oven to 325F and line a 9.8" x 13.7" (25cm x 35cm) baking pan with parchment paper.
2. In a large bowl, beat softened butter with low carb sugar substitute and cream cheese until fluffy.
3. Add one egg at a time, almond extract, vanilla extract, orange liquor, if using, and beat until well combined.
4. In a separate bowl, combine dry ingredients: almond flour, coconut flour and baking powder.
5. Add dry ingredients slowly to the wet ingredients and blend until well combined. This is where you wrap your "coin" (we use a quarter) with aluminum foil and mix it into the batter with a spoon or spatula.
6. Pour cake batter into the lined baking pan and spread evenly.
7. When baking this cake for a New Year's Day celebration, with the sliced almonds, decorate the top of the cake forming the numbers of the upcoming year or "Happy New Year".
8. Bake for about 50-60 minutes, until it is golden brown, and the toothpick you insert comes out clean.
9. Remove from the oven and allow to completely cool.
10. Once cooled, sift your choice of powdered sugar substitute to decorate your cake.

MACROS: (per piece)
Calories: 360.2
Fat: 31.7 g / 78.2%
Protein: 10 g / 11.6%
Net Carbs: 4.24 g /8.9% (if you omit the orange liquor: 3.90g /8.6%)

For optimal results don't use a larger baking pan otherwise your vasilopita will be too thin.

ELIOPSOMO / GREEK OLIVE BREAD
My Greek Keto Kitchen: Desserts and Breads

Dairy Free

Prep Time: 30 minutes
Cook Time: 70 minutes
Servings: 18 slices about 1cm each

This homemade Greek olive bread screams "Greek and delicious"! You won't believe that this is grain-free, gluten-free, sugar-free and guilt-free! Serve with your favourite dip, turn into a sandwich or simply do what any Greek does... dip it into a Greek salad to absorb all the juices from the tomatoes and olive oil! The choices are limitless!

Ingredients:

- 2 cups (224 g) almond flour
- 1/4 cup (45 g) psyllium powder
- 1/2 tsp sea salt or pink Himalayan salt
- 1 tbs baking powder
- 1 tbs garlic powder
- 1/4 cup (60 ml) Greek extra virgin olive oil
- 4 large eggs (beaten)
- 15 Kalamata olives (Pitted and diced)
- 1/2 cup (118 ml) boiled water, slightly cooled

Baking Method:

1. Pre-heat oven to 350F. Line a 9x5 loaf pan with parchment paper.
2. Boil water and allow to slightly cool, but it needs to be hot.
3. In a large bowl mix all the dry ingredients (almond flour, psyllium powder, baking powder, garlic powder and salt) together with a spoon or spatula.
4. Slowly stir in one at a time, the eggs, olive oil, olives and finally the hot water. Mix well to create air bubbles that are the sure sign of a well baked bread.

5. Allow the dough to rest for a few minutes.
6. With wet hands, transfer the dough to the prepared loaf pan and form into a rounded loaf.
7. Bake for 55-70 minutes. It not only needs to pass the toothpick test, but we are looking for a crisp hard crust that is a nice light brown. Cool completely before removing from the pan.
8. Enjoy warm or at room temperature! Store this bread in an airtight container in the fridge (if not consumed the same day) for 7 days or freeze it in a freezer-safe container up to a couple of months. Re-heat in the oven and enjoy!

MACROS: (per slice)
Calories: 141.8
Fat: 11.2 g / 71.5%
Protein: 4.2 g / 12%
Net Carbs: 1.91 g / 16.5%

ELLINIKES PITES / GREEK PITA BREADS
My Greek Keto Kitchen: Desserts and Breads

Dairy Free

Prep Time: 40 minutes
Cook Time: 30 minutes
Servings: 6

These homemade pita breads are easy to make and are simply delicious! You won't believe that these are grain-free, gluten-free, sugar-free and guilt-free! Oh, and depending on how you cook them, dairy-free too! Serve them with your favourite dip or turn them into a sandwich, stuffed with souvlaki, meatballs - the choices are limitless! I am providing two choices, one using coconut flour and the other almond flour, I wonder which will become your absolute favourite?

Ingredients for 6 coconut flour pitas:

- 1/2 cup (70 g) coconut flour
- 1 tbs psyllium powder (use 2 tbs for a chewier dough)
- 2 pinches of sea salt or pink Himalayan salt
- 1 cup (250 ml) boiled water, slightly cooled
- 1/2 tsp dried oregano
- 1 tsp garlic powder

Ingredients for 6 almond flour pitas:

- 1 cup (112 g) almond flour
- 2 tbs psyllium powder
- 4 pinches of sea salt or pink Himalayan salt
- 3/4 cup (180 ml) boiled water, slightly cooled
- 1/2 tsp dried oregano
- 1 tsp garlic powder

Baking Method:

1. Boil water and allow it to slightly cool, but it needs to be hot.
2. Mix all the dry ingredients together with a spoon.
3. Slowly add in the hot water, while mixing with a spoon. It will form into a ball. *If needed, add a bit more water but be cautious. We are looking for a Play-doh consistency. **Almond flour absorbs differently than coconut flour so, add hot water slowly to get the right consistency of a dough.**
4. Allow the dough to rest for about 5-10 minutes – if using oven method pre-heat your oven to 350F while waiting.
5. Separate the dough into 6 portions by forming balls. Roll out the dough between two pieces of parchment paper or use a tortilla maker, but still use two pieces of parchment paper. Roll or flatten as thin as you can without the dough breaking.
   TIP: when you use wet hands to roll, it is much easier to form the dough into balls.
6. You can bake them for about 15-20 minutes or until slightly golden brown at 350F on a prepared baking sheet. Halfway through baking, flip the pitas and rotate the baking sheets from top to bottom rack for an even baking. A watchful eye is necessary to not over-bake them. You can also cook them in a skillet by lightly brushing the pan with butter, coconut oil or avocado oil using medium heat. Cook them for a couple of minutes on each side until golden brown.
   TIP: you may need to adjust the heat on the stove top to medium low as your pan heats up.
7. Enjoy warm or at room temperature! Store these pitas in an airtight container in the fridge (if not consumed the same day for 7 days) or freeze them in a freezer-safe container up to a couple of months. Re-heat in the oven and enjoy!

MACROS for 1 Coconut Flour Pita:
Calories: 82.1
Fat: 4.9 g / 53.2%
Protein: 1.7 g / 8.2%
Net Carbs: 2.09 g / 38.7%

MACROS for 1 Almond Flour Pita:
Calories: 165.9
Fat: 13.8 g / 74.9%
Protein: 4.1 g / 10%
Net Carbs: 2.03 g / 15.1%

You may attempt using other spices or herbs such as mint, parsley, thyme and basil.

Macros are including about 2 tbs of butter when using butter to cook pitas in a skillet. I prefer this baking method; however, it is a personal choice.

BEVERAGES

GREEK FRAPPÉ / FREDDO ESPRESSO / FREDDO CAPPUCCINO
My Greek Keto Kitchen – Beverages

Dairy Free   Nut Free

It may come as a surprise that Greece has a huge coffee culture that begins from the times of its Independence in 1821. Wherever you go in Greece, you will find a Kafeneio (coffee house). There are traditional ones where the clientele consists mostly of the town's male elders drinking their coffee with friends and neighbours, while playing Tavli (similar to backgammon) or holding their komboloi (worry beads). The more modern upscale coffee shops are mostly a gathering of friends who meet up for every possible occasion. Greeks find any reason to get out and about, and socialize!

*If you have ever been to a Kafeneio in Greece or in your local Greek restaurant, you might have noticed that there is a special way to order your coffee. Your choices consist mainly of **gliko** (sweet), **metrio** (medium sweet) and **sketo** (unsweetened). Truth be told, my choice was always **gliko**, that was until I began my Keto Journey. Before long, my taste buds changed and the need for sugar has disappeared, so now, it's strictly **sketo** all the way!! Additionally, I always loved my frappés - especially on those hot summer days. Recently however, after visiting Greece, we saw a huge new trend towards Freddo Espresso and Freddo Cappuccino that definitely caught my attention. So, I definitely had to experiment and now, I share these recipes with you!*

> *NOTE* Use 1 tbsp for **metrio** (medium sweet) 2 tbsps for **gliko** (sweet), however, sweeten to your liking with a low carb sugar substitute or omit completely (**sketo**).*

Ingredients for Frappé:

- Instant Coffee (if you can find the traditional Greek Nescafé great, if not any good quality will do)
- Monk fruit & erythritol blends are Keto-friendly (feel free to use your choice of low carb sugar substitute, however, optional)
- Water
- Your choice of heavy cream, unsweetened almond, cashew, coconut milk (optional)

- Cinnamon (optional)
- Ice Cubes
- Frother (stand up or hand milk frother)
- A tall glass and a straw

Preparation:

1. Place 1tbsp of instant coffee in your tall glass.
2. Add your choice of low carb sugar substitute if using (see NOTE above for amounts).
3. Add a couple of pinches of cinnamon, if using.
4. Pour a little water (no more than 2 fingers width and just enough to cover the dry ingredients.
5. Place glass under your stand up frother or place hand frother in your glass and blend until the froth has reached about halfway up your glass.
6. Add 4-5 ice cubes to your glass.
7. Pour water slowly into your glass as you see the froth rise. Allow a little space if you are adding a "milk" (choices above).
8. Add your desired "milk" slowly into the glass if using (I used 2 tbsp of heavy cream).
9. Insert a straw, stir and enjoy!

Ingredients for Freddo Espresso:

- A bit more than 3/4 cup (0.85 cup) (200 ml) (or 2 double shots) of espresso coffee or strong brew of coffee ** I used 200 ml*
- Monk fruit & erythritol blends are Keto-friendly (feel free to use your choice of low carb sugar substitute, however, optional)
- Water
- Cinnamon (optional)
- Ice Cubes
- Blender
- A [a heat resistant glass or tall cup] glass and a straw

Preparation:

1. Prepare your espresso or brewed coffee, as usual.
2. Add 2 ice cubes to a blender and add only 1/4 cup or 50ml of your prepared coffee.
3. Add your choice of low carb sugar substitute, if using (see NOTE above for amounts).
4. Add a couple of pinches of cinnamon, if using.
5. Blend on high for only a couple of seconds or until most of the ice is crushed and the coffee becomes frothy.
6. Pour the frothy mixture into a heat resistant glass or tall cup and add a couple more ice cubes.
7. Slowly add in the remainder of the prepared coffee. You will see the froth rise as you add the coffee.
8. Insert a straw, stir and enjoy!

Ingredients for Freddo Cappuccino:

- A bit more than 3/4 cup (0.85 cup) (200 ml) (or 2 double shots) of espresso coffee or strong brew of coffee *I used 200 ml*
- Monk fruit & erythritol blends are Keto-friendly (feel free to use your choice of low carb sugar substitute, however, optional)
- Water
- Your choice of heavy cream, unsweetened almond, cashew, coconut milk (I used heavy cream as I enjoy a thick froth)
- Cinnamon (optional)
- Ice Cubes
- Blender and Frother (stand up or hand milk frother)
- A [a heat resistant glass or tall cup] glass and a straw

Preparation:

1. Prepare your espresso or brewed coffee, as usual.
2. Add 2 ice cubes to a blender and add only 1/4 cup or 50 ml of your prepared coffee.
3. Add your choice of low carb sugar substitute if using (see NOTE above for amounts).
4. Add a couple of pinches of cinnamon, if using.
5. Blend on high for only a couple of seconds or until most of the ice is crushed and the coffee becomes frothy.
6. Pour the frothy mixture into a heat resistant glass or tall cup, and add a couple more ice cubes.
7. Slowly add in the remainder of the prepared coffee. You will see the froth rise as you add the coffee.
8. Pour 1/3 cup (about 78 ml) of heavy cream into another glass or shaker and place under the stand up frother or place hand frother in your glass/shaker and whirl/blend for about 1-3 minutes. We are looking for a nice frothy consistency. If you are not using heavy cream, use 1/2 cup (about 118 ml) of any other non-dairy substitute as listed above.
9. Slowly pour into the prepared frothy coffee mixture, and watch the magic happen.
10. Insert a straw, stir and enjoy!

MACROS: (per Frappe coffee)
Calories: 102.8
Fat: 10.8 g / 92.6%
Protein: 0.9 g / 3.6%
Net Carbs: 0.91 g / 3.8%

NOTE *Macronutrients are based on using heavy cream and a couple of pinches of cinnamon.

MACROS: (per Freddo Espresso)
Calories: 3.2
Fat: 0 g / 0%
Protein: 0 g / 0%
Net Carbs: 0 g / 0%

From Left to Right
GREEK FRAPPÉ /
FREDDO ESPRESSO /
FREDDO CAPPUCCINO

MACROS: (per Freddo Cappuccino)
Calories: 256.5
Fat: 26.9 g / 92.4%
Protein: 2.4 g / 3.9%
Net Carbs: 2.13 g / 3.7%

ELLINIKOS KAFES / GREEK COFFEE

My Greek Keto Kitchen – Beverages

Dairy Free   Nut Free

*Let's not forget our beloved traditional Greek coffee. Making Greek coffee is simple, but it demands a specific brewing technique with distinctive characteristics. This strong coffee with foam on top is brewed by using a **briki** (a long handled pot with a pouring lip) and is poured into 2 side-by-side **demitasse cups** (also known as espresso cups). What makes Greek coffee unique is that the coffee beans are ground to a fine powder that eventually settles to the bottom of the cup. What it creates is **a thick coffee liquid gold** that is thick and strong. The rich foam that develops and gently rises to the top is called **kaïmaki (pronounced kaee-MAH-kee)**. Greek Coffee is usually served with a glass of water and a little sweet treat. You may also add sugar to the coffee while it is brewing. Keep in mind the 3 distinct styles of preparing Greek coffee: the **vari gliko** (very sweet), **gliko** (sweet), **metrio** (medium sweet), **sketo** (unsweetened).*

> *NOTE* 1tsp. for **metrio** (medium sweet) 2tsp. for **gliko** (sweet), 3tsp. for **vari gliko** (very sweet), however, sweeten to your liking with a low carb sugar substitute or omit completely (**sketo**)*

*Ingredients for Greek Coffee (yields 2 demi-tasse cups): ***These are not your traditional measurement cups***

- Greek Coffee
- Water
- Monk fruit & erythritol blend (feel free to use your choice of low carb sugar substitute, however, optional)
- Briki
- Greek Coffee Cups (or demitasse cups also known as espresso cups)

Preparation:

1. Measure out 2 portions of water by filling up the cup that you are using (demitasse cup, or Greek coffee cup, or espresso cup, which all measure around 2 ounces). Pour the 2 portions of water (about 4 ounces) into your briki, and ensure that there is enough space for it boil up and create a foam.
2. Add 2 tsp of coffee and your preferred amount of "sugar" if using (look at NOTE above for amounts) for every 1 cup of coffee you are making and stir. Remember that we are making 2 cups of coffee, so in this instance 4 tsp of coffee and your desired amount of sugar substitute, if using is all you need. This is considered a strong ratio for coffee.
3. Place the briki on low heat and let it come to a boil very slowly. NB: Do not leave the coffee unattended and keep a close eye on it to ensure that the foam does not over-boil.
4. Stir occasionally, and until the mixture starts to rise (picture a volcano waiting to explode). Once it starts foaming, lift it off the heat so that the foam settles. Then return it to the heat and let it start foaming up again. Then, remove it once the foam starts to rise. This method is important to follow carefully to yield a great brewed coffee. You don't want to over-boil it, otherwise it will not have that creamy foam top, and under boiling it would allow for coffee grounds to not have settled and affect the taste experience.
5. Serve it by slowly pouring a little foam first, into the cups, and then pouring the remaining coffee.

MACROS: (per Greek Coffee)
Calories: 3
Fat: 0 g / 0%
Protein: 0 g / 0%
Net Carbs: 0 g / 0%

GREEK TEAS: MOUNTAIN TEA / TSAI TOU BOUNOU, SAGE / FASKOMILO, CHAMOMILE / CHAMOMILI

My Greek Keto Kitchen – Beverages

Dairy Free

Nut Free

*Greek herbs, including those used for teas, grow abundantly across the country. Depending where they grow in Greece, they are often given different names. The most commonly used ones are Mountain Tea (**Tsai tou Bounou**), Sage (**Faskomilo**) and Chamomile (**Chamomili**).*

Greek Mountain Tea is made from the dried leaves and flowers of the sideritis plant (or the ironwort plant), which is found high up in the mountain tops, hence, its name. It has been used since ancient times for aiding in digestion, the common cold or flu, aches & pains and is also known to alleviate anxiety.

Greek Sage (Salvia Fruticosa) is known for its healing benefits and known to be an anti-inflammatory and anti-bacterial. It is also used to relax an upset stomach and achy muscles. It is found in very dry and rocky areas.

Greek Chamomile (Chamaemelum nobile) can be found in abundance along the Greek countryside and in many people's gardens. This popular tea is used for many remedies such as stomach aches and bloating. It is universally known to help with sleep and has a mild sedative property that aids in relaxation. A cup is ideal right before bedtime. As a tincture, it is also known to benefit mild skin conditions, such as eczema or diaper rashes. I remember my mother healing a rash by steeping chamomile leaves and soaking a cotton pad to use as a compress.

Ingredients for 1 cup of tea:

- Your choice of loose tea leaves
- Monk fruit & erythritol blend to add some sweetness. Feel free to use your choice of low carb sugar substitute.
- 1 cup of water
- A kettle [or saucepan – old school]

Preparation:

1. Using the loose dried tea leaves of your choice, remove 1 to 2 stems and crush them gently.
2. Fill your kettle [saucepan, teapot] with water and turn the heat to medium-high.
3. Drop your tea leaves into the pot and bring to a boil.
4. Once boiling begins, remove the pot from the heat and allow the tea to steep for about 5 to 7 minutes.
5. Using a fine strainer to remove the tea leaves, carefully pour the tea into a cup.
6. Add your choice of low carb sugar substitute, if using. Enjoy!

MACROS: (per Greek Tea)
Calories: 0
Fat: 0 g / 0%
Protein: 0 g / 0%
Net Carbs: 0 g / 0%

From Left to Right:
SAGE / FASKOMILO
CHAMOMILE / CHAMOMILI
MOUNTAIN TEA / TSAI TOU
BOUNOU

Sharing My Personal Favourites
My Greek Keto Kitchen

As a Certified Ketogenic Nutritional Coach, I am constantly reading and learning new topics on health & wellness. On a personal note, I have always been a health advocate and love reading anything on the subject! Through this journey, I have discovered many experts and authors within the Keto Community that I highly recommend. The following is a list of well-known and respected professionals from around the world who speak from experience and expertise. I am proud to say that I have had the privilege to meet some of these amazing people and continue to be inspired by them. I am thrilled to share them with you!

Jimmy Moore, to whom I send a big shout out as the man who inspired my husband and I to take a leap of faith and begin this lifestyle that literally changed our life for the better. As a family we had the opportunity to meet Jimmy Moore in person and thanked him for sharing his personal journey with us, and he was gracious enough to autograph his book, ***"KETO CLARITY"***, which he co-wrote with Eric C. Westman, MD. This was the very first book that I read back in 2014 when my husband brought the Keto Diet to my attention. This is a well-written book that will easily guide you through a Ketogenic Diet and inspire you to embrace this lifestyle. Their other writing collaboration, ***"CHOLESTEROL CLARITY"***, is a great companion on your Keto journey, and will provide you with information that explains that "cholesterol is not actually bad" for you. Jimmy Moore continues to educate, motivate and encourage others in their personal wellness journeys.

You can follow ***Jimmy Moore*** on Instagram @livinlowcarbman and learn more about him at www.livinlavidalowcarb.com

Dr. Eric C. Westman is the co-author of **"KETO CLARITY"** and **"CHOLESTEROL CLARITY"** and adds his expertise and knowledge as a physician and globally renowned researcher in low-carb ketogenic medicine by presenting the science behind this lifestyle. I had the privilege to meet Dr. Westman at the Keto Summit in 2018, where he also kindly autographed his **"KETO CLARITY** for us. Furthermore, Dr. Westman shares his knowledge through YouTube, where he has over 100 free educational videos on various topics covering the Ketogenic Diet.

You can follow **Dr. Eric C. Westman** on Instagram @ecwestman and @adaptyourlife as well as on YouTube under "Adapt Your Life"

Dr. Eric Berg, DC is a chiropractor and health educator specializing in nutrition. After years of continuous research and from personal experience, he has dedicated himself in helping others achieve overall health in a simple way. He shares his extensive knowledge through his health education videos on YouTube where he has over 3M subscribers and over 2K free videos. In his book **"THE HEALTHY KETO PLAN"**, he writes about the principles of eating a healthy keto diet, intermittent fasting and much more. I received my **Ketogenic Nutritional Coach Certification** from Dr. Berg, and I am humbled and grateful to call him my mentor. I had the privilege to meet Dr. Berg at his Keto Summit in 2018.

You can follow **Dr. Eric Berg** on Instagram @drericberg and YouTube under "Dr. Eric Berg DC"

Ivor Cummins, BE(Chem), CEng MIEI is a top engineer within his field of building medical and other industry devices. He is known for leading worldwide teams in complex problem-solving initiatives. He has taken his years of technical expertise and chose to devote it towards researching the root causes of chronic disease, such as cardiovascular disease, diabetes and obesity. Ivor Cummins now shares his research and knowledge at various public speaking events such as the one I had the opportunity and pleasure to attend, Dr. Bergs Keto Summit in 2018. At this event, he discussed his findings on nutrition, chronic disease and specifically fat and cholesterol. His book ***"EAT RICH LIVE LONG"***, (co-authored by Jeffry Gerber, MD who is a preventative medical expert), outlines the details and results of their scientific research, and how to prevent and heal chronic disease.

You can follow ***Ivor Cummins*** on Instagram @thefatemperor and learn more about him at www.thefatemperor.com

Dr. Ken D. Berry, MD is a family physician who specializes in overall optimal health and disease prevention for over a decade. His main focus and mission have been to put a stop to chronic illnesses such as type 2 diabetes and chronic inflammation. After starting this particular research, he decided to make healthier changes in his life. When these changes presented measurable results, he began sharing his discoveries with his patients so that they could benefit as well. While in his practice and during his research, Dr. Berry began collecting all the lies and myths that either he or other doctors were telling patients. From all that he learned and uncovered, he wrote his book ***"LIES MY DOCTOR TOLD ME"***. This is a great book that helps us realize that we need to take our health into our own hands and do our own research. This book also uncovers the truths of our health care system that may need to be overhauled if we wish to create more health and less illness.

You can follow Dr. Ken D Berry on Instagram @kendberry.md and YouTube under "KenDBerryMD"

Nina Teicholz has an extensive and impressive career as a renowned leader in nutrition reporting. Specifically, she is an investigative science journalist, speaker, researcher, professor (adjunct) at NYU, Executive Director of The Nutrition Coalition, and a New York Times bestselling author of *"THE BIG FAT SURPRISE"*. Her book is full of studies, articles, citations and more, and it highlights evidence that dietary fat is not bad for us. Nina Teicholz's 9-year investigation reveals the truth about fat and that everything we were told was a lie. On a personal note, I do have to mention that Nina Teicholz's husband is Greek, and Greek cuisine is among her favourites. She has also written for various magazines and newspapers reviewing restaurants, and she definitely knows what she likes.

You can follow *Nina Teicholz* on Instagram @ninateichols and learn more about her at www.ninateicholz.com

Recipe Index
My Greek Keto Kitchen

MEZEDES - APPETIZERS

KEFTEDAKIA-
GREEK
MEATBALLS
p.28

MELITZANOSALATA
– EGGPLANT
SALAD (DIP)
p.31

SKORDALIA –
GARLIC MASH
p.34

TIROKAFTERI,
KOPANISTI, HTIPITI
SPICY CHEESE DIPS
p.37

DOMATOKEFTEDES -
TOMATO FRITTERS
(KEFTEDES)
p.41

TZATZIKI - CUCUMBER,
GARLIC & YOGURT
GREEK DIP
p.44

KOLOKITHOKEFTEDES
- ZUCCHINI FRITTERS
(KEFTEDES)
p.47

SALADS - VEGETABLES

SALATA
KOUNOUPIDIOU -
CAULIFLOWER SALAD
p.51

PRASINI SALATA
FASOLION - GREEN
BEAN SALAD
p.54

ELLINIKI SALATA ME PIPERIES
STI SKARA - GREEK GRILLED
PEPPER SALAD
p.57

ELLINIKI SALATA ME
KRITHARAKI - GREEK
ORZO SALAD (FAUX)
p.60

ELLINIKI SALATA ME
KOLOKYTHAKIA STI SKARA -
GREEK GRILLED ZUCCHINI SALAD
p.63

HORIATIKI
SALATA -
GREEK SALAD
p.66

RADIKIA (HORTA)
SALATA - DANDELION
(GREENS) SALAD
p.69

TRADITIONAL DISHES

BIFTEKIA -
GREEK
HAMBURGERS
p.73

SOUVLAKI - GREEK
PORK ON A SKEWER
p.76

PASTITSADA,
KOKKINISTO - VEAL POT
ROAST & STEWED VEAL
p.79

KOTOSOUPA ME
AVGOLEMONO - CHICKEN
SOUP with LEMON SAUCE
p.82

MOUSSAKA - MEAT
EGGPLANT
CASSEROLE
p.86

PASTITSIO -
MEAT AND
FAUX PASTA
CASSEROLE
p.91

SOUTZOUKAKIA -
GREEK
MEATBALLS IN A
TOMATO SAUCE
p.96

SPANAKORIZO -
SPINACH RICE
p.100

SPANAKOPITAKIA -
SPINACH PIES
p.103

TIROPITAKIA -
CHEESE PIES
p.107

Recipe Index
My Greek Keto Kitchen

DESSERTS - BREADS

AMYGDALOTA - GREEK
ALMOND COOKIES
p.112

GALAKTOBOUREKO
- CUSTARD PIES
p.115

KOULOURAKIA - GREEK
BUTTER COOKIES
p.118

KOURABIEDES - GREEK
SHORTBREAD COOKIES
p.121

RAVANI - ALMOND
COCONUT CAKE
p.124

VASILOPITA - GREEK
NEW YEAR'S CAKE
p.127

ELIOPSOMO - GREEK
OLIVE BREAD
p.130

ELLINES PITES -
GREEK PITA BREADS
p.133

BEVERAGES

GREEK FRAPPÉ -
FREDDO ESPRESSO -
FREDDO CAPPUCCINO
p.138

ELLINIKOS KAFES
- GREEK COFFEE
p.143

GREEK TEAS - MOUNTAIN TEA - TSAI
TOU BOUNOU, SAGE - FASKOMILO,
CHAMOMILE - CHAMOMILI
p.146

Printed in the USA
CPSIA information can be obtained
at www.ICGtesting.com
LVHW081510090124
768362LV00029B/1674